Anita Theis

A forecast on the development of the 3D TV market in the US

Will 3D TVs become the next big thing in our living rooms?

Anchor Academic
Publishing

Theis, Anita: A forecast on the development of the 3D TV market in the US: Will 3D TVs become the next big thing in our living rooms?. Hamburg, Diplomica Verlag GmbH 2013

ISBN: 978-3-95489-000-2
Print: Anchor Academic Publishing, an Imprint of Diplomica® Verlag GmbH, Hamburg, 2013

Bibliographical Information of the German National Library:
The German National Library lists this publication in the German National Bibliography. Detailed bibliographic data can be found at: http://dnb.d-nb.de

The digital publication (eBook) of this work with the ISBN 978-3-95489-500-7 can be purchased on the general market or directly from the publisher.

EXECUTIVE SUMMARY

This research study answers the question of whether 3D TV will become a new trend or if it is a hype that will eventually fail to establish itself.

The paper is divided into a market research and a target group research. Both deal with the situation within the United States as the US has one of the highest market shares in 3D globally.

3D TV was introduced in 2010 and within that year the 3D TV sales made out 4% (3.2mio) of all TV sales. Within the US, 3% of the households purchased a 3D TV so far. According to E. Rogers' book "Diffusion of Innovation" whose theory is used as a guideline throughout the whole research paper, those 3% make out the category of innovators.

In order to reach out to other categories of the adopter categorization as well, the 3D TV technology has to face economic, sociological and technological challenges. Those challenges as well as the trends and developments influence the adoption of the technology. Those influencing aspects can be grouped into five categories: relative advantage, compatibility, complexibility, observability and trialability. The research determines how the different aspects concerning the 3D technology influence these categories in order to come up with possible forecast of 3D TV.

The relative advantage is mainly influenced by the target group's perception of 3D TV. While 3D TV aims to add an experience domain to the traditional experience of 2D TV, this is not especially valued among the target group. The price of 3D TV sets however does play a significant role – many consider the prices of 3D as too high. However the experience teaches that the prices are likely to decrease due to the price setting strategy called "price-skimming". The most important factor concerning compatibility is the unfavorable launch-date of 3D TVs in the US. In 2010 most people have just bought an HDTV and now are satisfied with the technology they have and do not see any reason to buy a new TV any time soon. Other factors influencing the compatibility are the need to wear glasses, which are expensive and uncomfortable. Also the digital revolution plays a role – TVs in general lose their influence while computers with the help of internet have the role of a multi-media device that makes TVs redundant. On the positive side, the increased production of 3D content that fits the target group's profile makes 3D perfectly compatible with the target group's values.

Though 3D TV is a rather complex technology, especially a this time now that there is new technology developed all the time, creating an information jungle – the target group research shows that the target group is surprisingly well educated about the technology and that this education positively influences the perception towards 3D TV. Trialability/Observability – those two categories are grouped together within the research. Outside of the movie theaters, the trialability/observability is pretty limited . However there is a positive correlation between trialability/observability and the perception towards 3D. That shows that the people that actually have the chance to watch 3D at some place do like it and have an increased probability to purchase a 3D TV.

In the end and compared with the target group research, it seems as if the 3D TV technology will actually make it and become a new trend.

PREAMBLE

This research study would not have been possible without the help and the endless support of my friends, family and the team behind Story House Productions in Washington, DC.

Conducting an extensive research study such as this one cannot be done without a group of people that offers support – not only concerning the needed knowledge, but also mentally. Therefore, this paper will never be a work that has been done all by myself, but was only possible with the help of a lot of people.

First of all I want to thank the team of Story House Productions in Washington, DC for giving me the great opportunity to work with and for them, and for all the knowledge and competences that I have gained.

I want to thank Katharina Osterholt for not only being a great friend during hard times, but also for sharing knowledge and in being an awesome motivator.

James P. Tanabe – not only for proof-reading, but also for your belief in me and your great friendship!

There were a lot more people that have supported me in different ways and without whom I would not be where I am right now.

I want to thank everyone who believed in me – even at times when I did not.

Anita Theis

CONTENT

LIST OF ABBREVIATIONS

CTAM - Cable & Telecommunications Association for Marketing

HDTV – High Definition Television

LCD – Liquid Crystal Display

LED – Light-emitting Diode

VOD – Video on Demand

INTRODUCTION

The 3D technology is almost as old as the movie theaters and was invented by Charles Wheatstone in 1838. His discovery was followed by the production of the very first 3D movies in 1922 (Zone, 2007, p1). But despite of its early invention this technology had to go through a lot of ups and downs, changes and improvements for almost 90 years, before it made its debut to where TV established itself in the 1920s: the consumers' living rooms.

2010 was the year in which the third dimension was introduced to private homes and has not been restricted to the movie theaters anymore ("An introduction to 3D Television", 2010). Today, in 2011, the 3D technology is improved continuously in order to satisfy the consumer. But that does not make it easier to introduce it to the target group: Constant changes and developments create an information jungle for the consumer who therefore lacks the knowledge to make a well-informed decision about adopting to the technology. Because of that the danger is that 3D TV will fail to reach out to the broad mass.

PROBLEM STATEMENT & MAIN QUESTION

The major TV manufacturers such as Sony, Samsung, Panasonic or Toshiba introduced their first 3D TV sets in early 2010 reaching out to a global target group.

By the end of 2010, studies conducted by the Nielsen Company and Renub Research showed that only 2% of the US citizens have bought a 3D TV – globally a total of approximately 3.2 million 3D TV sets were sold, making out 4% of all TV sales in 2010.

The forecasts of 3D TV have been very ambivalent throughout: While some predictions expect 3D TV to become a major success for the entertainment industry and the new standard in the consumers' living rooms within the next three to five years, other studies however conclude that the introduction of 3D TV had been too early and call it a hype that soon will be forgotten.

By taking the theory about diffusion of innovation into account, it seems the 3D TV technology has only been adapted by the category of innovators so far – the first 2.5% of people that adapt to a new product or technology. Several different reasons could account for the slow adoption rate: from the consumer's perception of 3D TV to the challenges that this new market has to face.

At the same time however, the investment into 3D TV is high for both TV manufacturers as well as 3D content providers. Their challenge is to increase the adoption and reach out to a broader target group in order to turn 3D TV into a successful new niche product that has the chance to become a new trend and a new standard.

The key to success lies in the consumer – only if they are convinced of the new technology they be triggered to adapt to it.

This research is therefore determined to find an answer to the question of whether or not 3D TV will be able to increase its adoption among the target group and therefore become successful within the next 3 to 5 years.

This research is basically divided into two parts: Part 1 consists of an in-depth market and desk research of 3D TV and includes the challenges, trends and developments of this technology. Part 2 consists of a target group research that carrier the assumptions and conclusions of the market research part further and tests those on the target group directly. The results of both research parts then together will be able to answer the main question.

RESEARCH QUESTIONS

Several research questions were set up in order to find an answer to the main question of this research.

Part 1:

1. What is 3D TV?
2. What is the extra value of 3D TV?
3. What is the market position of 3D TV as of early 2011 in the United States of America?
4. What are the challenges of 3D TV?
5. What are the trends and developments of 3D TV up to Qt1 2011 worldwide and with a special focus on the US?
6. How does the adoption process of a new technology usually progress and how did the adoption process of the 3D TV technology progress in the US since its introduction in 2010?

Part 2:

7. How does the target group's perception towards 3D TV influence the adoption rate of 3D TV?

JUSTIFICATION OF RESEARCH

This research provides an in-depth insight into the market situation of 3D television and both its challenges and developments. This is complemented by a target group research about the consumer's perception of 3D TV and the possibilities of increasing the adoption of this innovation. By providing insight into different studies that have been conducted about 3D TV, this research paper unravels all the available information and puts them into a new light to give an indication whether 3D TV will make its way to ubiquity or oblivion.

Everett M. Rogers (Diffusion of Innovation, 2003, 5th ed.) defined five characteristics that influence the adoption rate of an innovation. Based on his book, this dissertation determines in how far those characteristics favor or disfavor the adoption process of 3D TV and how current trends and developments within the 3D TV sector might improve this process. These conclusions are then used in a target group research in order to determine whether they are feasible and will lead to a higher adoption rate of the technology within the next 3 to 5 years.

In this regard, this research paper can act as a guide for both TV manufacturers and TV content producers that invest or plan to invest into 3D TV.

However, the main purpose of this paper is to become the starting point for marketing managers of those companies that already have their stakes in 3D technology; this research gives insight into how the adoption process can be improved and therefore it can be used as a foundation of a successful marketing plan.

METHODOLOGY

DATA USED

This research study is based on primary, secondary and tertiary data.

TERTIARY INFORMATION

Tertiary information that is for this dissertation are databases such as LexisNexis and summaries of papers or market researches, when the access to the full information had been limited or restricted due to the costs of such an access.

SECONDARY INFORMATION

The first research part consists of thoroughly researched information that was found in both print media and online media, accessible for a low or small budget and which was then analyzed in the light of the problem statement and main question of the paper. This information consists of up-to-date sources about 3D TV as well as theory of marketing, strategy and economy. Additionally, results of research e.g. MarketSearch, DisplaySearch and Nielsen were taken into account as secondary data.

PRIMARY INFORMATION

After the analysis of tertiary and secondary data, primary information for the second part of this paper was gathered by conducting a survey among the target group. By gathering primary information, it became possible to get results that exactly match the problem statement of the research. A detailed explanation of the methodology used for the target group research can be found in part 2 of this research paper.

CONSTRAINTS AND LIMITATIONS

Several limitations and constraints should be taken into consideration when reading through this research study.

BUDGET

This is a fully independent and non-financed research. There has been no budget available in order to conduct the research. However, the access to publicly available papers by market research companies cost between $1,500 and $10,500. As it has therefore been impossible to gain full access to those papers, this research relies to some extent on summaries of the above mentioned studies instead of official data.

CONSTANT CHANGES IN THE SECTOR

As 3D TV is a relatively new technology which is going through a lot of developments and changes, new information might have been released during the time this research was set up, conducted and analyzed. Though this research paper aims to give insight into the latest developments of 3D TV, some of the information laid out might not be up-to-date anymore at the time the paper is published. All information has been taken into account as of March 2011.

PART 1 –DESK-RESEARCH

RESULTS

The following chapter will answer the research questions of part 1 of the research.

WHAT IS 3D TV?

HOW IS THE 3D EFFECT CREATED?

3D refers to anything that has height, width and depth. The human eye itself however sees only height and width – 2D. The reason that we experience the surrounding world with a 3D effect is due to our brain. The human's eyes are about 2.5" (6.5cm) apart from each other, so that each of the two eyes sees an object from a slightly different angle at all times (Koninklijke Philips Electronics N.V. [Philips], "What is 3D?"). The brain takes those two images and processes what we see into a 3D view: a 2D world with depth as an added dimension.

Modern 3D technology tries to achieve the same effect by showing two separate images, one to each eye at a time. By converting those two images together such as in "real life", the brain creates the 3D effect for us. This is called stereoscopic 3D (Media College, "What is 3D?".) and is often referred to as the "real 3D", because there are also different ways to create 3D effects synthetically.

3D – FROM 1838 TO 2010

After the discovery of 3D by Charles Wheatstone in 1838, different feature films for 3D were developed with a major emphasis on the gimmicks that this new technology offered, for example objects that seem to fly towards the audience (Zone, 2009, p.1). But the 3D technology experienced its first real boom when more than 50 3D movies were produced between 1952 and 1955. The second boom of 3D occurred in 2005 with the release of the first digital projected 3D movie "Chicken Little 3-D". But a new milestone in the history of 3D movies and a breakthrough of this technology occurred with the launch of James Cameron's blockbuster "Avatar" (Sander, 2009) – the most successful movie in history. It even surpassed Titanic which held this position since 1997 (Box Office Mojo, "All Time Box Office – Worldwide Grosses").

The booms of 3D movies in the 1950s and around 2000 had a specific reason: the everlasting competition between the movie theaters and home TVs (Mendiburu, 2009):

In the 1950s and 1960s a major development for TVs was when color TV sets were introduced globally, turning TV into the major competitor for the traditional movie theaters. People started to value watching TV at home more than going to expensive movie theaters. In order to gain back their market share, the theaters therefore had to come up with a new competitive advantage: the 3D technology (Mendiburu, 2009, p6-7). Back in the 50s and 60s, the 3D technology has obviously not been fully developed yet and 3D was shown in color anaglyph, requiring the audience to wear the well-known red/cyan or red/blue plastic glasses. Nevertheless - it created new revenues and the cinemas were once again filled with a huge audience. But the appearance of the Digital Revolution changed the TV sector once again: home entertainment, video-on-demand

and file sharing became another stroke in the competition between TVs and cinemas. Those developments in home entertainment gave the consumer the freedom to watch whatever he liked whenever he wanted to. This resulted in a decrease of revenues for the cinemas once again and built the basis for the need invest into the production of a new generation of 3D which eventually lead to the next boom of 3D. A lot of money was invested for the production of new and better technology with the aim to create a better experience and an added value for the consumers.

3D COSTS AND REVENUES

3D in the cinemas stands for "Dollars, Dollars, Dollars": During opening weekends, a 3D movie makes three times the revenue of a 2D movie. But yet, all 3D movies that are released need a supplementary 2D version in order to pay for the costs. So far there are not enough 3D capable theaters in order to pay for all the costs (Mendiburu, 2009, p4).

Any new technology, product or service on the market should have at least one relative advantage to other similar products/services/technology in order to attract customers. The same goes also for the 3D TV technology. This paragraph unravels the unique selling point (USP) of the new 3D TVs.

Not only does 3D add depth as a third dimension to the TV experience – but by imitating the natural vision of the human eyes, 3D increases the immersion of the audiences and therefore positively improves the affect of identification and projection. By providing 3D images to the consumer, less brain activity is necessary. This results in a more immerged audience that can enjoy more of the TV watching activity (Mendiburu, 2009).

There are four experience domains described by Pine and Gilmore, differentiated by two variables: the degree of participation (passive or active) and the consumer's relation to the environment (absorption or immersion). An experience belongs to at least one of these domains but is considered to be stronger and more valuable if it consists of more than just one domain (Nijs & Peters, 2006).

The four domains are:

1. Entertainment
2. Educational
3. Esthetic
4. Escapist

(Pine & Gilmore. 1999, p 30 - for the graphic please refer to graphic 5 in appendix 1)

Usually, watching TV is an activity in which the consumer absorbs the movie passively – which is why watching TV is considered to belong to the domain of Entertainment. With the introduction of 3D however, the same activity becomes more immerging and adds Esthetic values to the experience.

The domain of esthetic is characterized by style, beauty, art, etc. and a passive consumer who cannot interact with what is going on (Nijs & Peters, 2006). Or as Pine and Gilmore summarize:
"*While guests partaking of an educational experience may want to* ***learn****, of an escapist experience to* ***do****, of an entertainment experience want to—well,* ***sense*** *might be the best term—those partaking of an esthetic experience just want to* ***be*** *there.*" (Pine & Gilmore, 1999, p35)

Watching 3D TV therefore creates a more valuable and memorable experience for the audience than traditional 2D movies and shows.

The perception however about what is a valuable experience cannot solely depend on theories like that alone: it depends always on the consumer's perception. That is why the target group research in part 2 should give a more accurate answer to the question if 3D TV is able to create a more valuable experience compared to 2D TV.

WHAT IS THE MARKET POSITION OF 3D TV IN THE US?

In early 2010 the world's biggest TV manufacturers such as Samsung, Sony, Toshiba and Panasonic launched the first 3D home TVs in the new market.

A market research conducted by Renub Research called "3D TV Market and Future Forecast Worldwide (2010 - 2014)", published on January 19, 2011 at www.marketresearch.com expected a total of 3.2 million 3D TV sets to be sold globally in 2010, a number that makes out 4% of all TV sets sold in the same year. Additionally, their forecast for the 3D TV market expects the unit sales to grow with a compound annual growth rate of 79.12%, passing the landmark figure of $100billion worldwide by 2014 (Market Research, 2011).

A report published by Display Search called "Quarterly TV Design and Features Report, Q4 2010" expects 18million 3D TV sets to be sold in 2011 and 90 million by 2014. With a combined market share of 66.17%, the USA and South Korea are the main protagonists on the 3D TV market (Display Search, 2011; Gagnon, 2009; Tribbey, 2009).

The United States are a potentially big market for 3D TV: 115 million homes out of a total of 130million (U.S. Census Bureau, 2010) have at least one TV – a total of almost 88.5% of the households. The average US household is equipped with 2.5 TV sets while almost a third of them (31%) have 4 TVs or even more. According to the Nielsen's National People Meter (NPM) from September 2010, the "average American" spends 25.6 hours per week watching TV (The Nielsen Company, 2011 - see also graphic 6).

These numbers show clearly that the USA has a great potential and a wide and diverse target group to introduce 3D TVs to. Nielsen's NPM and Nielsen's Global Survey from September 2010 also indicate a percentage of 46% of all Americans who own an HDTV of which 14% are connectable to the Internet. Their data also show that 2% of the Americans have already purchased a 3D TV with a total of 2million 3D ready HDTVs being sold in North America in 2010 (The Nielsen Company, 2011)[1]. Those percentages indicate that there is not only a broad target group for new technologies, and that the group of innovators within the States already adapted to this new technology.

CONSUMER'S ATTITUDE TOWARDS 3D

According to a large scale quantitative research with consumers, conducted by CBS Vision together with Nielsen and CTAM, consumers are generally positive towards 3D TV: 76% of the surveyed people state that they are at least likely to buy a 3D TV, 17% of which are even "definitely" likely. However only 14% intend to buy a 3D TV within the next 12 months, another 42% want to wait at least 2 years and 34% want to wait three to four years. So even though the consumers are generally positive towards the new technology they are not yet ready to adapt to it. 48% find watching 3D content more engaging than 2D and 57% say that it made them feel like being part of the action and

[1] Data from Nielsen's Global Online Survey conducted 09/2010. Nielsen surveyed 26,644 online consumers ages 15+ in 53 countries. This numbers only include US and Canadian consumers.).

another 48% state it makes them feel closer to the characters (The Nielsen Company, 2010)[2].

THE CHALLENGES OF 3D TV

3D TV as a new product in the market faces a diversity of challenges. According to the PESTEL model, challenges can be divided into **p**olitical, **e**conomic, **s**ocial, **t**echnical, **e**nvironmental and **l**egal challenges (Johnson, et al., 2008).

When analyzing the 3D TV technology, the most important challenges can be grouped into sociological, technological and economic factors. The sociological challenges probably have the greatest influence on the adoption of 3D TV as those deal with the potential consumers' perceptions and concerns and the marketing strategies of the 3D industry. On the other hand, technological problems and challenges need to be faced in order to make 3D TV more successful. The following paragraph analyzes those challenges in detail in order to come to a conclusion in how far which aspect needs to be improved in order to increase the adoption of 3D TV.

The major challenges on the 3D market that will be discussed are:

- Economic Challenges
    - Costs
    - Launch-Date
- Technological Challenges
    - Standardization of technology
    - 3D glasses
    - Lack of content
- Sociological Challenges
    - Consumer's wait-and-see approach
    - Education of consumers
    - Mistaking the 3D effect by 3D producers

[2] Nielsen Wire – quantitative and qualitative research conducted in collaboration with CBS Vision and the Cable & Telecommunications Association for Marketers (CTAM) among 12 groups and families being exposed to 3D content for 30 minutes at Sony's 3D Experience Lab in Las Vegas plus an additional 425 participants watching 3D content in a more theatrical surrounding. Results published on December 20th, 2010 at www.nielsen.com

ECONOMIC CHALLENGES

COSTS

Both the production of 3D content as well as the manufacturing of 3D displays is more expensive compared to their 2D counterparts. The costs of 3D movie productions are up to four times the costs of the same movie produced in 2D (Mendiburu, 2008). And at the end the consumers have to pay for these extra costs. Even though the prices dropped drastically since the introduction of 3D TVs in 2010, 3D sets are still more expensive than 2D sets. Also, in order to watch 3D at home - to buy just the 3D TV is not enough. The consumer needs to buy a whole set, consisting of the 3D display, a 3D BluRay Player, a transmitter and 3D glasses. All of that added together makes the 3D experience at home a rather expensive one. Especially for large households the 3D experience can get really expensive because they need to purchase multiple pairs of 3D glasses. And as long as the active shutter glasses (around $120 per pair) are the most widely used- this can sum up to become a huge investment just in order to watch 3D at home.

UNFAVORABLE LAUNCH-DATE

The introduction of 3D TVs to the North American market occurred after the majority of the household adapted to HDTV. Apparently some 21% of all US households bought a new TV within the last 12 months and consider themselves set with their TVs. Only 18% of the households plan to purchase a new TV within the next 12 months (Entertainment Marketing Letter, 2011). This unfavorable launch date of 3D TV might explain a low adoption of the technology.

TECHNOLOGICAL CHALLENGES

STANDARDIZATION OF TECHNOLOGY

There is neither a defined standard for 3D TV production right now but there are also a lot of different technologies on the market. The consumer has the choice between active or passive 3D TVs, maybe at some point even auto-stereoscopic 3D TVs; he has the choice between LCD or Plasma displays and much more different options. Even though it seems that there should be technology to fit all the different types of consumers, this huge choice actually creates an information jungle, confusing the consumer. The usual consumer is hardly able to keep up with all the latest developments and changes of the technology and therefore becomes confused. This confusion can lead to some sort of frustration that leads to the fact that the consumer develops a wait-and-see-approach (see sociological challenges - consumer's wait-and-see-approach) and hesitates to adapt to the 3D TV technology.

3D GLASSES

3D glasses are a challenge for the 3D TV technology in different ways.

According to studies conducted by the Nielsen Company together with CTAM, the main reasons the target group named about why they do not buy a 3D TV are: costs (68%), and the need to wear 3D glasses (57%) (Nova Gazette, 2010).

The most widely used 3D TV technology is active 3D that requires so-called active shutter glasses in order to see the 3d effects. Those glasses cost – depending on the manufacturer – between $100 and $150 per pair. But those glasses only work with a 3D display from the same manufacturer and are not compatible with a 3D TV from another brand. That means that a consumer who decides to purchase a 3D TV from one brand and at some point might want to buy a new one from another brand, the glasses become useless. It also makes it impossible to "just bring your own pair of 3D glasses" to someone else's place and watch 3D TV there together if this person does not have a 3D TV from the same brand.

According to the Nielsen&CTAM research, it is not only about the price of those glasses but the consumer also considers them to be very uncomfortable.

LACK OF 3D CONTENT

Even though the different manufacturers develop more and more 3D TVs of all sizes, the 3D content still pretty much limited to 3D movies that are available on DVD. For the consumer this obviously is a major issue that makes them hesitate to buy a 3D TV (Shein, 2010). According to The Nielsen report about the consumer's perception towards 3D TV the Top 3 of content they want to watch in 3D are Sports, Nature/Animal and Action/Adventure shows (The Nielsen Company, 2010, see graphic 11).

CONSUMER'S WAIT-AND-SEE APPROACH

Due to former format battles such as the battle between Plasma vs. LCD displays or BluRay vs. HDTV – consumers learned to not adapt to a new technology that is available on the market right away. They tend to wait until there is one "winner"; one clear format that gets implemented for mass production to which the consumer then adapts, in order to rashly adapt to a technology that might fail in the end (Stagliano quoted in Entertainment Marketing Letter, 2011).

Yet another reason that contributed to the consumers' wait-and-see approach was Toshiba's announcement in 2010 to launch its first auto-stereoscopic (means: glasses-free!) 3D TV worldwide during the second half of 2011 (Lilly, 2010). As seen earlier, the 3D glasses are of a great disadvantage for the 3D experience – so the idea of eventually having a 3D TV soon that does not even require glasses at all anymore, leads to a consumer who is happily waiting for this improvement of the technology before he goes and settles for a 3D TV that will not completely satisfy his needs, while a glasses-free 3D TV will bring an essential advantage. Additionally, the consumers are aware of the fact that if they wait until the technology settles, the prices will drop. In that case that means instead of purchasing a 3D TV now – if they wait some more time they will get a better product for a cheaper product. This is called delay of gratification and increases the consumer's wait-and-see-approach.

So while the consumer might be interested and excited about this new technology – he is not yet ready to buy (The Nielsen Company, 2010).

This is also the reason why only innovators and early adopters are likely to adapt to a new product/technology during its first phases of the product-life-cycle, while the mass waits and needs to be persuaded of it by strategic marketers.

NOT SUFFICIENTLY EDUCATED CONSUMERS

One problem of the 3D industry is still that the potential consumer just knows too little about the technology and the possibility that it holds. A lot of people seem to be unaware of the fact that a 3D TV does not mean that you can only watch 3D content on it, but that it works as a very good 2D HDTV (Roberts, 2010). The manufacturers therefore need to concentrate on selling the 3D technology not only as a 3D TV itself but as a high-quality HDTV with the ability to also show 3D content.

MISTAKING THE EFFECT OF 3D

This challenge refers mainly to the 3D content producers. A danger of producing 3D is to think that everything that is made in 3D will attract the consumers. However, people go and see movies or shows because of the content, the story and the concept – not because they want to "see technology". The 3D technology adds a new dimension to the experience of watching TV, but does not create a completely new experience as it is not standing on itself but acts as an addition to something that already exists. Therefore for 3D the same rules apply as they do for 2D – in order to get people behind the screen there needs to be a good concept and a good story, and a bad 2D movie will not make a good 3D movie either - but a good 2d movie might become more attractive in 3D (Mendiburu, 2008). Humans seek per definition for diversification (Nijs & Peters, 2006). They are attracted by 3D because it adds a thrill to their experience if e.g. objects are flying towards them. The challenge for 3D producers is to combine the experience-domain-adding gimmicks with the essential part of a good story-telling (Mendiburu, 2009).

TRENDS AND DEVELOPMENT OF THE 3D TV MARKET

The following paragraph deals with the current trends and developments on the 3D TV market as of March 2011:

- New 3D content on the market
- New technology
  - Passive 3D TVs
  - Auto-stereoscopic 3D
- Universal 3D glasses
- Decreased prices
- 3D Online-Streaming Services

3D CONTENT

Though so far there is only a limited amount of 3D content, within the next few months there will be more than 40 new 3D movies released and additionally, some TV shows starting in 2011 will also be available in 3D. Combined with a great number of sport events broadcasted in 3D, both networks and production studios spend a huge amount of money in order to make more 3D content available for the customer (Oshannessy, 2010).

Also several broadcasting channels unveiled their plans on launching 3D based channels in 2011 – all of which together help to broaden and diversify the available 3D content for the consumer.

Some examples are:

3Net – on February 13, 2011, 3Net was launched, a joint venture of Discovery, Sony and IMAX, offering 3D content 24/7 (www.3net.com).

XFinity 3D - launched on February 10, 2011 by Comcast. A 24/7 3D channel that broadcasts concerts, sport events and movies (Inside Satellite TV, February 18, 2011).

ESPN 3D - launched by Comcast in June 2010. They broadcasted some of the 2010 World Cup matches live in 3D and nowadays broadcast diverse sport events live such as boxing, golf or NBA games (www.espn.com).

3D TVS

As 3D TVs are still new to the market, a lot of improvements and changes are constantly made to this technology. The two most important developments of 3D TV technology are discussed here.

AUTOSTEREOSCOPIC 3D TVS

Auto-stereoscopic 3D refers to a new technology in the 3D sector which does not require the need to wear 3D glasses in order to see the 3D effects. This technology is already used for the new Nintendo console, the 3DS, which was launched in North America, Europe and Australia in early 2011 for a retail-price of $249,99 (www.nintendo.com). Also LG uses this technology with the world's first auto-stereoscopic 3D cell phone, the Optimus 3D (www.lg.com).

After Toshiba announced their plans in 2010 to launch the first auto-stereoscopic 3D TVs worldwide in late 2011, they started introducing the first 3D TVs without glasses in Japan on December 22, 2010. For about $3,400 the consumers can buy a 12" or a 20" 3D TV for which they do not require 3D glasses (www.toshiba.com). Despite the presentation of larger auto-stereoscopic 3D TVs at the CES in Las Vegas in 2011, there is no indication to be found on how much progress they made for their planned global introduction.

Even before Toshiba's announcement of launching glasses-free 3D TVs, Philips has already started producing those displays but discontinued the production due to a slow adoption rate, stating that the market is not yet ready for this technology (www.philips.com).

PASSIVE 3D TVS

The most widely used type of 3D TVs are active displays that require active-shutter glasses which use a transmitter to be synchronized with the TV.

Less common – because they are new to the market - are passive 3D TVs that work with cheap polarized plastic glasses that are available for much under $50. Hereby, the TV itself has a thin layer over the standard display, made up of incredibly thin magnifying strips that show a slightly different perspective of the screen to each eye and therefore create the 3D effect (Sniderman, 2011).

The advantage of passive 3D displays is a less dimmed image. Because this technology uses polarized plastic glasses without any shutter, the picture appears brighter with a decreased ghosting effect. Also there is no need for a synchronizing transmitter so there is no possibility to have a flickering affect with passive TVs (Werner, 2011).

On the downside, passive displays have a smaller resolution compared to active 3D sets because each eye only sees half of the screen and the picture quality therefore is not quite as good comparatively speaking. This loss of quality however might not even be visible to the regular audience and only be recognized by more experienced and concerned viewers (Werner, 2011). Therefore a passive 3D TV might be a good solution for e.g. families that decide to switch to 3D TV as they do not the face of buying a lot of expensive active-shutter glasses.

PRICES

New technology usually gets introduced to the market at a relatively high price during the first stage of its life cycle – the so-called price skimming strategy – in order to be able to drop prices as the product matures so that it can reach out to all of the segments of the consumers (Djolov, 2006). While the price difference between a 2D and a 3D TV was several thousand dollars at the beginning of 2010, the price difference decreased to only a couple of hundred dollars today (Oshannessy, 2010) due to the increased competition in the 3D TV market. Though there are obviously no maximum limits to what a consumer could possibly pay in order to buy a 3D TV, there are 3D displays available for less than $1,000. A 3D BluRay Player, which is needed to watch 3D content, is available for under $200 and a transmitter to synchronize the active shutter glasses with the display will cost around $50, along with the glasses of around $150 per pair [3] (www.bestbuy.com).

So a full 3D set for home-usage can be purchased for a retail price of under $1,500. Comparatively speaking, at its introduction in 2010 the 3D screen itself cost around $3,500. That makes the purchase of 3D TV sets today quite affordable and some experts even say that the prices are as low as they will probably ever get (Oshanessy, 2010).

3D GLASSES

The 3D industry has to deal with what causes major concerns among the consumers – the 3D glasses. Not only that they are perceived as being uncomfortable and expensive, they are also not compatible with displays of another brand.

There are several companies on the market that put their effort into developing universal 3D glasses that work with a wide range of brands. Among those is RealD: they recently introduced a new and universal 3D glasses technology that accepts input from different 3D TVs via different means of communication. With this technology, the consumer would not be dependent on a specific brand of glasses anymore. However, RealD also announced that they will start production starting quarter 2 in 2011 and it might still be a long way until this new technology will make its way to mass production and consumer sales (Greenwald, 2011).

[3] Prices as seen on www.bestbuy.com on March 10, 2011: Sony Bravia 32" 3D LED-LCD HDTV for $899,99; Sony 3D InternetConnectable Wi-Fi Ready Blu-ray Disc Player for $179,99; Sony Bravia Battery Operated 3D glasses for Sony 3D Flat-Panel HDTVs for $149,99; and Sony 3D sync Transmitter for $49,99

3D ONLINE STREAMING

The streaming service offered by Wal-Mart, called Vudu, announced plans on offering 3D streaming services directly to an internet-connectable 3D TV. For $4.99 the consumer can watch the latest 3D movies via online streaming – such as Step Up 3D, Monster House 3D, Bolt 3D, Meet the Robinsons 3D or Chicken Little 3D (www.vudu.com).

The well-known streaming and DVD delivery service Netflix however does not offer 3D streaming possibilities, but they added 3D titles into their collection for regular DVD delivery which can be ordered for no additional costs (www.netflix.com).

The following chapter will explain the consumer-adaption-process of an innovation such as a new product or technology according to Everett Roger's consumer-adoption-process model he developed in his book "Diffusion of Innovations" (2003, 5th edition).

3D TV is considered to be an innovation, even though 3D itself is not a new technology. But nonetheless, most people have usually not yet dealt with the possibility of watching TV in 3D and therefore this is a new technology and considered to be an innovation.

According to Rogers, the adoption of an innovation follows the innovation-decision process: The process in which the decision is made of whether to adopt or to reject an innovation via five steps: knowledge of an innovation, persuasion, decision, implementation and confirmation. An individual gains knowledge of an innovation after which he forms an attitude towards it. In the following he either makes the decision to reject the innovation or adapt to it and make full use of it (Rogers, 2003). This process is illustrated in graphic 8, appendix 1.

Individuals however do not adapt to an innovation all at once – they differ in the time they need to pass through the process from knowledge phase to adoption/rejection. Rogers refers that to an individual innovation-decision period. The rate of adoption of an innovation is usually measured by the length of time that is required for a certain percentage of the members of a social system to adapt to an innovation. Rogers defines five groups that are distinguished by their level of innovativeness: "the degree to which an individual is relatively earlier in adoption to new innovations compared to others in the social system." (Rogers, 2003)

1. Innovators
2. Early Adopters
3. Early Majority
4. Late Majority
5. Laggards

For Rogers' adopter's group categorization with percentaged distribution please refer to graphic 9 in appendix 1.

The rate of adoption is affected by different characteristics which are helpful in predicting people's reaction to an innovation. Those five characteristics will be taken into account when analyzing how the latest trends and developments can face the current challenges of 3D TV in order to increase the adoption rate.

I. **Relative advantage** – the degree to which an innovation is perceived better than the idea it supersedes
II. **Compatibility** – the degree to which an innovation is perceived as consistent with the existing values, past experiences and needs of potential adopters
III. **Complexity** – the degree to which an innovation is perceived as relatively difficult to understand and use
IV. **Trialability** – the degree to which an innovation may be experimented with on a limited basis

V. **Observability** – the degree to which the results of an innovation are visible to others

(Rogers, 2003, p223-258)

ANALYSIS

This analysis is determined to figure out how the trends and developments of 3D TV can overcome the challenges of the market and therefore possibly improve the adoption according to the five characteristics that influence the adoption of an innovation.

RELATIVE ADVANTAGE

The aim of the 3D TV technology is to create a more memorable experience of watching TV by including an esthetic experience to the entertainment domain. If this is successful and the consumer values the added experience this would lead to a higher adoption rate. In order to figure out the consumer's perception however, a separate target group research needs to be conducted (see part 2 – target group research).

Another factor that can become a relative advantage are the costs of 3D TV that so far negatively influenced the adoption of 3D TV. The market research showed that the prices of 3D displays decreased immensely since the introduction of 3D TV which might be able to favor the purchase of 3D TV. This however is only possible if the consumer is actually educated about this development. Due to the fast pacing 3D TV market the consumer tend to not be up-to-date with the latest developments and therefore probably do not know that 3D TV sets are not as expensive as they might think they are.

Yet a third aspect able to influence the relative advantage is the need to wear 3D glasses which are not only uncomfortable but also very expensive. The development of passive 3D TVs (lighter and cheaper glasses), the development of universal glasses (compatible with more than just one brand of 3D TVs) and the introduction of auto-stereoscopic TVs in the near future can take away this barrier and therefore another negative factor on the relative advantage perceived by the consumer. For this aspect it is also important to take a look at the level of awareness and knowledge of the consumer regarding 3D technology, as this factor can only improve the relative advantage if the target group is fully aware of that.

We can conclude that the adoption rate of 3D TV can be increased by improving the relative advantage if:

a) The target group values the added experience domain of esthetic to traditional 2D TV.
b) The costs do not longer build a barrier that hinders the target group of switching over to 3D TVs.
c) 3D glasses become cheaper or get substituted at all by auto-stereoscopic 3D TVs
d) The target group is fully educated about the changes in the market and values them.

In general the reason to watch TV is amusement, either in order to become more educated or to relax. 3D TV logically aims to fulfill the same needs and values of the consumers and is therefore generally compatible with the consumers' expectations.

On the down side however, one main challenge of 3D TV is the consumer's wait-and-see approach, meaning that the consumers tend to wait until the technology has settled. The fact that there is not yet one standardized technology for 3D fortifies this approach and therefore makes it hard to overcome. Together with the unfavorable launching date of 3D TV to a market that is essentially saturated with TVs makes it hard to be compatible with the needs of the target group at the moment.

Additionally, the lack of 3D content negatively influences the adoption of 3D TV as so far there is only little content available. But as more and more movies are produced in 3D and several broadcasting channels launched their first 3D channels during the last couple of months and even streaming/VOD-services extended their 3D offers, more content becomes available for the consumer.

As a conclusion about the compatibility of 3D TV, there is some limitation about how much this can be increased in order to increase adoption of 3D technology. The unfavorable launching date will probably result in an adoption that occurs later than originally hoped for, and as about the standardization of the technology, this obviously will not change soon. Too high is the competition on the market and too young the technology as there will be a clear standard in a nearby future. However the development of universal glasses might be the first step into the right direction.

More available content could definitely trigger the consumer to adapt to 3D TV, but it will depend on whether or not the upcoming releases are conform with the target group's value to different types of content they wish to see. And again it is subject to the question of whether or not the target group is informed about the developments in the market for it to become successful.

COMPLEXIBILITY

Due to the different technologies on the market and the constant changes make 3D TV a rather complex technology that might be perceived difficult to understand by the consumer. The consumers are not very educated about the opportunities and the different types of 3D TVs and the technology behind it. This might be a characteristic of 3D TV that negatively influences the adoption rate of 3D TV.

Better marketing techniques to educate the consumers together with a standardized technology might be helpful to take away this obstacle of the consumer.

TRIALABILITY/OBSERVABILITY

Regarding the activity to watch 3D TV we will summarize both trialability (the degree to which the consumer can try out an innovation) and observability (the degree to which the target group can observe an innovation) into one category. Trying out and observing 3D TV content results in the same activity.

As seen from the results of the market research the actual number of American households that already possess a 3D TV is very low. This fact limits the trialability of the 3D TV as the potential consumer is not able to have a look into the technology at e.g. friends' or co-workers' places either. However, this does not mean that there is no way to get to know the 3D technique at all. Many multimedia stores, such as Best Buy, have 3D TVs in display as a marketing instrument. There the consumer can experience 3D TV and additionally can be advised by experienced staff if he wants to get to know more. Additionally to the trialability and observability possibilities at multimedia stores there is of course also the high number of 3D movies shown at the cinemas. The high number of recently released or planned 3D movies might act as a trigger for the consumer to purchase a 3D TV in case the 3D experience in the cinema makes him develop an increased value for 3D technology.

CONCLUSION

The main purpose of the market research was to determine which factors play a significant role for the adoption process of 3D TV and which of the current trends and developments could possibly overcome the challenges of the market. Those results will then be used to determine how likely that is with the help of a corresponding target group research.

After the desk research we can conclude a number of barriers that might negatively influence the adoption of 3D TV. Those critical success factors need to be overcome and communicated well-enough to the target group in order to make 3D TV successful.

These are

- Extra added value
- Costs/Price
- 3D glasses
- Content
- Standardization of technology

Some of the major challenges that play a significant role for the adoption process of 3D technology can be overcome with the current trends in the market: Prices already dropped a lot and might drop even further. Expensive active shutter-glasses will be substituted by either universal glasses that at least will not only work for one brand of 3D TVs anymore or by cheap plastic glasses for passive 3D TVs or – in a not yet determined future – become unnecessary with the introduction of auto-stereoscopic 3D TVs. At some point the goal will be to have one standard of the technology, though that might take some more years, but then it will become easier for the consumer to understand the technology und unravel the information-jungle for them making it easier to adapt to the technology. Additionally by taking the forecasts for 3D sales into account, it will become easier for an interested person to try out the technology as the number of households that possess a 3D TV will increase, making this innovation more accessible and also easier to understand.

The following target group research will determine the target group's perception towards 3D TV and how they perceive both the challenges and the trends of the market in order to come up with a conclusion whether the adoption of the technology is indeed about to increase or not.

PART 2 – TARGET GROUP RESEARCH

RESEARCH DESIGN & METHODOLOGY

PROBLEM STATEMENT

The preceded market research about 3D TV technology showed that the adoption of 3D TV so far has only reached out to the innovators, as only 2% of the Americans purchased a 3D TV since its introduction in 2010. The industry's goal however is to increase the adoption rate and to reach out to the next categories of adaptors.

This target group research is therefore aimed to answer this question:

How does the target group's perception towards 3D TV influence the adoption rate of 3D TV?

TARGET GROUP

This target group is aimed to reach out to the potential target group of 3D TV with a special emphasis on the innovators and early adopters. First of all a definition of the innovators has to be made in order to get to figure out how they are characterized. Defining this group can be made by an in-depth analysis of specifically the group of people that states that they do already possess a 3D TV.

As a second step the research will have a look at the early adopters as those are the next group of consumers that need to be convinced of this technology. E. Rogers compiled a list of characteristics for early adopters of a new technology, which will be used to reach out to the adequate target group for this research. Early adopters are considered to be opinion leaders that act as a role model within their social system, being able to help triggering the "critical mass when they adapt to an innovation" (Rogers, 2003).

General characteristics include (but are not limited to): a higher social status with a greater degree of upward social mobility, a higher ability to cope with uncertainty and risk, a greater exposure to mass media & interpersonal communication channels. Early adopters compared to later adopters also seek information about innovations more actively and have a greater knowledge about those (Rogers, 2003).

But even though the next task of the 3D TV sector will be to persuade the early adopters, the general aim is to reach out to a broader mass and include all of the potential consumers. This is why the target group of this research is held very broad in order to be a general foundation for 3D producers.

The target group will therefore include to both female and male American citizens between 18 and 65 years.

SAMPLE SIZE

In 2011, the American population was 308,745,538 of which 101,248,160 between 18 and 65 years of age (U.S. Census Bureau, 2011). This number is the total population out of which a sample size will be drawn.

The sample size to conduct a valid survey is calculated by using the following formula:

$N = p\% * q\% * [z / e\ \%]^2$.

- 'N' is the minimal size of the sample.
- 'p%' is the percentage of the specified category
- 'q%' is the percentage not belonging to the specified category
- 'Z' is the Z-value belonging to the required level of reliability
- 'e%' is the required error level

(Saunders, et al., 2004)

In order to reach the highest level of validity and reliability, the minimum sample size is calculated with a confidential level of 95% and an error level of 5%. This results in a sample size of 384 respondents.

ADJUSTMENT OF THE SAMPLE SIZE

Within the restrictions of time and the lack of any financial budget, it was not possible to get a sample size of 385 people. In order to deal with that, the error level has been adapted to the new circumstances. The total amount of respondents of 274 results in an error level of 5.9% and a confidence level of 95%.

Contrary to what was aimed at before conducting the research, the results might be a little bit less reliable and valid, but it still resembles a very high level of validity and reliability.

TOPICS

The following topics will be researched with the help of the target group research:

- Characteristics of the innovators of 3D TV
- The target group's household: size, occupation, children, income
- TV consumption and TV viewing behavior of the target group
- Interest and awareness of new technology in the (3D) TV sector
- Target group's perception towards 3D TV

RESEARCH QUESTIONS

In order to answer the problem statement of the target group research a number of research questions have been set up that will be answered by analyzing the results of the research.

1. How are the innovators of the 3D TV technology characterized?
2. What's the target group's TV viewing behavior and how affiliated are they with new technology in the TV market?
3. What is the target groups' perception towards 3D TV?
4. How educated is the target group about 3D TV?
5. What are the obstacles to adapt to 3D TV?

DECISIONS OF MAKING THE QUESTIONNAIRE

STATISTICS

Questions 1 to 9 are primary questions for statistical purposes, such as age, sex, state of residence, the educational level, occupation, household size and the household income. This data can later be used to describe the group of innovators as it can be cross-referenced to both the target's group perception towards the 3D TV technology and the question how the people are characterized that already own a 3D TV.

Those statistics will also be used to compare the sample of this survey to the actual demographic characteristics of the US population to give an estimate how reliable the results of this target group research are.

TV CONSUMPTION BEHAVIOR & TV TECHNOLOGY

The second section of the questionnaire deals with both the TV consumption behavior and the target group's interest in TVs and its technology. The question of what the consumer watches as well as how much TV they watch will be answered. Additionally, their buying behavior and their likeliness of buying (or not buying) a TV within the next two years can be answered and the reasons for that can be determined. As some theories say that one of the major flaws in the introduction of 3D TVs has been its unfavorable launch-date due to the fact that most people just recently bought an HDTV and therefore are unlikely to buy a new one, those questions aim to figure out if that is actually true.

How widely spread the adoption of HDTVs is can also be answered alongside with the question which kind of technology is usually used nowadays in the American households.

3D TV

The third section is about the 3D TV technology specifically. It is aimed to figure out how many of the people own a 3D TV to have a look if this percentage increased since the market research conducted by the Nielsen company.

Question 19 tries to figure out the general opinion of the target group towards 3D TV while in question 31 they are asked about where they think this technology will lead to. Question 30 asks which kind of content the target group wants to see the most. This is especially essential for broadcasting companies as they will not need to invest into an expensive technology if no one wants to see regular TV in 3D.

OBSERVABILITY & TRIALABILITY

Also the degree of observability can be found out by figuring out how easy the target group has access to a 3D TV by e.g. friends, family or other contacts. Also through cross-references the importance of observability/trialability can be figured out and how it increases the 3D perception or 3D buying behavior of the target group.

EDUCATION

Question 19, 23 and 27 deal with the education of the target group regarding 3D technology. It will be analyzed how much they actually know about the technology and how their degree of education influences both their perception and their buying behavior.

One major conclusion of the market research showed that the adoption of 3D depends to a large extent on the education of the target group regarding the 3D TV technology. New developments might be able to overcome the challenges that the technology faces nowadays but that is only possible if this is communicated well enough to the consumer. This point therefore plays a significant role in determining whether the adoption of 3D TV is likely to increase or not.

BARRIERS & OBSTACLES

Questions 24, 26 and 28 are aimed to figure out the major obstacles from a consumer's point of view towards 3D TV. It will be determined which the most important barrier to adapt to the technology is and also which of those obstacles – if eliminated – would most likely increase the consumer's perception of 3D TV.

TESTING OF THE QUESTIONNAIRE

Before sending out the final version of the survey, different people were asked to fill out several versions of the questionnaire for testing purposes. Their feedback had been analyzed and taken into account in order to optimize both the questions and their corresponding order within the questionnaire.

FIELDWORK

Two versions of this survey were designed in order to gather data from respondents: An online version and a hard-copy version.

ONLINE SURVEY

The main version is an online version of the questionnaire accessible via *www.thesistools.com/3dtv*.

This link was spread via different channels with the aim to reach out to as many people nationwide as possible:

At first the survey was send out by email to all accessible American contacts with the request to please fill out the survey and share the link to all of their contacts in order to spread the survey as widely as possible.

As a second step, social networks were used to spread the survey even further:

Advertisements were posted on craigslist (www.craigslist.com), the major American network for advertisements. Additionally, the link was posted on different social network sites, such as CouchSurfing (www.couchsurfing.com) and Facebook (www.facebook.com).

The advantage of making use of social networks is to reach out to a very broad group without any financial costs and with the ability to reach out to people from all over the nation with different educational backgrounds. On the downside however, the response rate of such an approach is fairly small and a lot of effort has to be made to reach out a lot of people in order to get the required amount of people to respond. Also, reaching out to a target group via social networks will result in a target group that does have certain characteristics such as a high affiliation to technology, especially the internet, and attracts mainly a younger target group.

PAPER VERSION

In order to increase the response rate a paper version was created and random people on the streets were kindly asked to fill out the questions of the survey - either by filling it out by themselves or by being asked the questions. This method has the big advantage that most of the people approached will be willing to invest 5minutes of their time if they are asked politely. Therefore this method leads to a high response rate. However, a great disadvantage is the time investment of this method and the fact that the people interviewed are limited to certain geographic restrictions and will not be representative for the whole nation. Therefore this method of collecting data will remain a secondary method while the main focus is on the online survey.
All information gathered by using the paper version of the survey has been manually entered online by the author to allow all data to be accessible centralized in one database.

PROCESS OF THE FIELDWORK

DETERMINING DATA

The target group used for conducting the research was held pretty broad by including both males and females between 18 and 65 years of age. This was especially important, because only by approaching a very broad target group there was the chance to reach out to some of the very few innovators of the 3D technology.

In order to get a reliable result, it was also aimed to get feedback from respondents all over the country and from all kind of different cultural and educational backgrounds. In order to conduct a research within such a broad target group the vast majority of the sample has been approached online by distributing the survey via different social media and by word of mouth marketing strategies.

CONTROL OF THE FIELDWORK

Control of the fieldwork was fairly limited due to the nature of online surveys. There is no way of determining whether someone entered the information truthfully or not. On the other side however, everyone gave away his or her data voluntarily so that there would have been no reason to fill out the survey if not with the premise to answer the questions correctly.

CONTROL WITH THE HELP OF ACCESSIBLE DATA

There are very up-to-date and complete data accessible about the demographic characteristics of the US population by the US Census Bureau. That information was used to compare the demographic information of the US population with the demographic data gathered in order to draw conclusion about the reliability of the data regarding the sample size.

BIAS

SAMPLE & SAMPLE SIZE

It was aimed to conduct the survey with a confidential level of 95% and an error level of 5% which would have lead to a fairly reliable result. However, due to time and budget constraints the required sample size of 385 respondents could not be met - leading to an adjustment of the error level to 5.9%.

Another limitation of the fieldwork was the ability to gain access to respondents that represent the US population as a whole regarding geographical, ethnic, educational and occupational backgrounds. The majority of the respondents of the target group research origin of the greater Washington DC area, they are fairly young compared to the median age and the majority is students living in a household that comprises of only one person. Those characteristics do not reflect the US population and falsify the results to some degree.

COMPARISON OF RESPONDENTS WITH ACTUAL DEMOGRAPHIC DATA

The following paragraph compares the demographic characteristics of the target group with the actual US population according to the U.S. Census Bureau and the CIA World Factbook.

The majority of the target group is between 18 and 33 years of age (see table 12) – compared to the median age in the US (36.8years), the target group of the research is comparable speaking younger than average. Furthermore the male-female-ratio is 52% to 47% (see graphic 10); this is slightly different to the American population with a ratio of 49% males and 51% females (Central Intelligence Agency, "The World Factbook – United States").

The majority of the researched target group resides in the greater Washington DC area and the neighboring States Virginia and Maryland with a cumulative percentage of 37.2%. Those States are represented above average while other States are under-represented or not represented at all due to the restriction in geographical distribution of the survey. No conclusion shall therefore be made in regards to the States of residence of the potential target group.

With 66.9%, the Caucasians form the majority of the target group (see graphic 7). This resembles to a great part the whole US population in which Caucasians are represented with 72.4% (Humes, 2011).

The majority of the sample are students with 19.9% (see table 13), explaining the relative young age of the target group and eventually influence the results of the survey as usually students do not have a lot of money to invest into technological gadget.

As we can see from that, the sample of the target group - does not really reflect the population of the United States. Though every action was taken to try to get an accurate and diverse sample - in the end the results of the research might be biased due to the financial restrictions of this research. If there is supposed to be a follow-up research it should be conducted with the possibility to actually reach out to a broader and more diverse target group.

CONSEQUENCES

The error level of this research is 5.9% instead of the 5% that was aimed for while the confidential level stays at reliable 95%. However the way the data was gathered resulted in a non-accurate demographic stratification of the target group so that it is preferred not to relate the results of the research with any demographic characteristic.

Also it has to be taken into account that the target group researched contains of a majority of students that might not have any financial possibilities to adapt to new technological innovations. Those constraints have to be taken into account when using the data for any other purpose.

RESULTS

This chapter answers all the research questions apart by analyzing the information gathered with the statistics program SPSS.

RESEARCH QUESTION 1 – HOW ARE THE INNOVATORS OF THE 3D TV TECHNOLOGY CHARACTERIZED?

The first research question provides a definition of the innovators of 3D TV by characterizing those people who already own a 3D TV.

Within the sample only 8 people stated that they possess an own 3D TV (3.1%). This percentage closely reflects the percentage found by other researches such as Nielsen and MarketResearch but it is difficult and not recommended to draw conclusions from a small number of respondents like this one as it will most likely not lead to any valid or reliable conclusions.

Of the people that own a 3D TV, all of them are males with the majority of 62.5% between 26 and 41 years (see table 14). 37.5% indicate to earn more than $150,000 (see table 15) and the vast majority works in the field of engineering/computer/technical (see table 16).

50% of the innovators attended some college and another other 50% have a master's degree or a Ph.D. 25% of the innovators have children under 18 living with them.

The innovators watch an average of 2h TV every day and half of the people purchased their last TV within the last 6months.

62.5% indicate that they also watched 3D content at friend's places within the last 12months, 28.6% watched 3D movies at the movie theaters.

Interestingly, their answer to the estimated price of a 3D TV set is not consistent (28.6% say under $1,000 and another 28.6% believe it costs more than $3,501) but the majority however (57.1%) think that the price of a 3D TV set is not appropriate.

As a greatest advantage of 3D TV the majority of 71.4% names the increased engagement into the action, and 57.1% say the biggest disadvantage is the need to wear glasses, 28.6% say it is the lack of content. No one mentioned the costs as biggest disadvantage of 3D Television.

The research shows that the majority of the innovators are interested to watch movies in 3D (85.7%), followed by Sports Events (71.4%), documentaries (57.1%) and animation content (42.9%). Interestingly none of the persons had an interest in watching reality shows or series in 3D, and also the News and Music shows rate low with both only 14.3%. (Comparing their answer to the question what type they usually watch, 100% answered to watch all of the options.)

Interest in watching in 3D:	Movies	Sports	Docus	Animation	News	Music	Reality	Series
%	85,7	71,4	57,1	42,9	14,3	14,3	0	0

TABLE 1 - INNOVATORS' INTEREST IN 3D CONTENT

RESEARCH QUESTION 2 –
WHAT'S THE TARGET GROUP'S TV VIEWING BEHAVIOR AND HOW AFFILIATED ARE THEY WITH NEW TECHNOLOGY IN THE TV MARKET?

Almost 90% of the target group does posses a TV, the majority of which possesses one TV (41.6%), one fourth (25.1%) possesses two TVs (see table 17). The majority watches less than 2h TV per day, and with 77.5%, the favorite content they watch are movies, followed by documentaries (61.6%) and the news (48.8%).

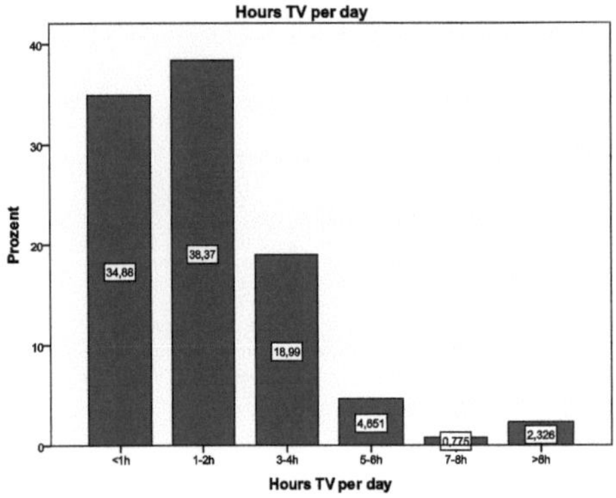

GRAPHIC 1- TV CONSUMPTION OF THE TARGET GROUP PER DAY

Movies %	Docus %	News %	Sports %	Reality %	Series %	Animation %	Music %	Other %
77,5	61,6	48,8	31,8	22,1	19,4	19,4	14,3	8,1

TABLE 2 – FAVORITE GENRES OF THE TARGET GROUP

More than half of the people indicate that they an HDTV, 24.8% of the TVs are internet-connectable (see table 18).

Most people (35.3%) purchased their last TV more than two years ago, 21.8% bought it within the last year (see graphic 12).

Only 19% say that they are at least somewhat likely to buy a new TV within the next two years – 34.9% say that they will definitely not do so (see table 19). As a reason for that, 60% state that they are currently satisfied with their TV and do not have a reason to buy another one. 22.9% state financial reasons and 18.2% say that they are not interested in the new technology that is available on the market (see table 20).

If they are asked what type of technology their new TV should have if they bought one, 40.7% say that it should be an HDTV, 31.4% want an internet-connectable TV and 10.4% are interested in a 3D TV (see table 21).

What is remarkable is the fact that half of the people is willing to pay only up to $500 for a new TV and less than 10% would pay more than $1,000 for a new TV (see table 22).

It is also interesting to have a look whether or not there is a correlation between the amount the target group is willing to invest into a new TV and the probability that they will buy a new TV within the next two years.

			Amount $ willing to invest in TV	Possibility to purchase TV next 2yrs
Spearman-Rho	Amount $ willing to invest in TV	**Correlation coefficient**	**1,000**	**,335****
		Sig. (2-tailed)	.	,000
		N	253	253
	Possibility to purchase TV next 2yrs	Correlation coefficient	,335**	1,000
		Sig. (2-tailed)	,000	.
		N	253	258

**. The correlation is significant at level 0,01 (2-tailed).

TABLE 3 - SPEARMAN CORRELATION: AMOUNT WILLING TO INVEST INTO NEW TV AND THE POSSIBLITY TO PURCHASE A NEW TV WITHIN THE NEXT 2 YEARS

The Spearman correlation coefficient in that case is 0.335 which indicates a light correlation between those two variables. Also the significance is below 5%, indicating a significant correlation. In that case it means that the more money the respondents are willing to invest the higher the willingness to buy a TV within the next 2 years.

The market research of 3D also indicated, that the slow adoption of 3D TV had been due to the unfavorable launch date of 3D TV because most people already bought a TV lately. Therefore we have a look at the correlation between the time the target group bought their last TV and their willingness to buy a new TV within the next two years. This will also be done by using Pearson Correlation.

			Possibility to purchase TV next 2yrs	When last TV purchase
Spearman-Rho	Possibility to purchase TV next 2yrs	**Correlation coefficient**	**1,000**	**-,112**
		Sig. (2-tailed)	.	**,071**
		N	258	258
	When last TV purchase	Correlation coefficient	-,112	1,000
		Sig. (2-tailed)	,071	.
		N	258	258

TABLE 4 - SPEARMAN CORRELATION: LAST TIME THE TARGET GROUP BOUGHT THEIR LAST TV AND THE POSSIBILITY TO PURCHASE A NEW TV WITHIN THE NEXT 2 YEARS

The correlation of -0.112 indicates a slight negative correlation between the time the target group purchased a TV and the possibility to purchase a TV within the next 2 years. Also the significance level is 7.1%, resembling no statistic significance between those two variables. This now means that the respondents that just lately bought a TV is less likely to buy a new TV soon. How that influences that actual 3D technology will be answered in research question 6.

RESEARCH QUESTION 3 - WHAT IS THE TARGET GROUP'S PERCEPTION TOWARDS 3D TV?

The target group was asked what they perceived as the biggest advantage of 3D TV. 114 out of 248 respondents (58.1%) say it is the increased engagement into the action and 18,1% state the picture quality is what they see as biggest advantage. While 21.4% stated that it is something different, most people who said that did not really state an advantage of 3D TV. Comments such as "I don't see an advantage" or "none" were the majority of those answers, just a few added that it is more entertaining and it would increase the gaming experience.

As seen in research question 1, the target group considers the same reason as greatest advantage as the innovators who have already adapted to the technology.

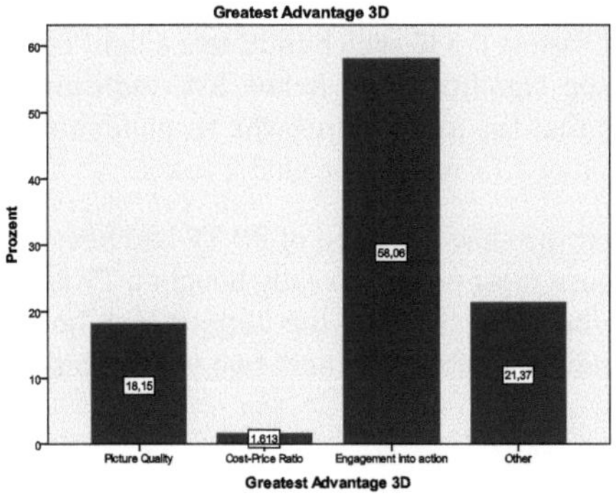

GRAPHIC 2 – TARGET GROUP'S GREATEST ADVANTAGE OF 3D

The general perception of the target group towards 3D TV (of only those that do not possess a 3D TV already) is mostly undifferentiated (48.26%), but another 35.2% have a negative perception compared to the 15.3% of the respondents that look more positive towards 3D TV.

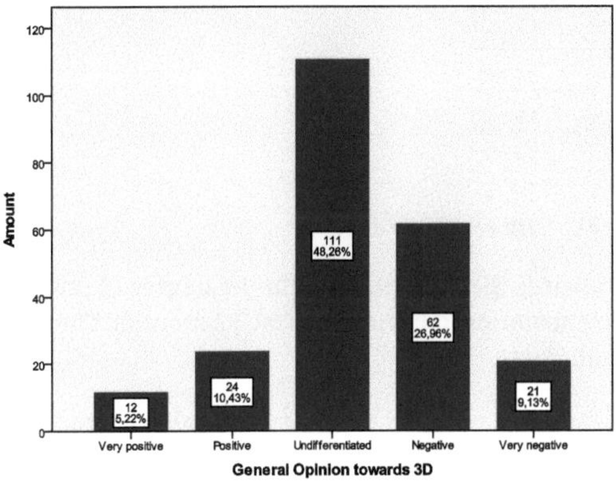

GRAPHIC 3 - GENERAL OPINION TOWARDS 3D OF THE TARGET GROUP

If we compare the target group's perception with the innovator's perception of 3D TV we see, that there is a big difference obviously. In this group, 85.72% have either a positive or a very positive attitude towards the 3D technology, with only 14.25% being rather undifferentiated. But none of those perceives 3D as negative.

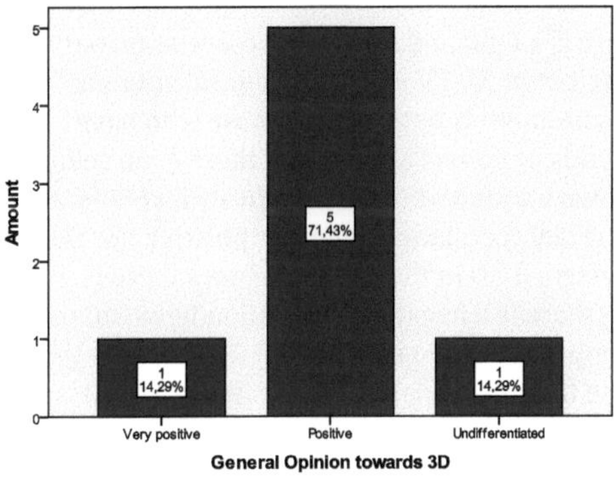

GRAPHIC 4 - GENERAL OPINION TOWARDS 3D OF THE INNOVATORS

Only a small amount of the target group – that means only the people that do not already have their own 3D TV – believe in 3D TV as a new trend soon (8.5%), 21.2% believe it will become a trend in a couple of year. Almost one fourth thinks that 3D will only remain a success in the movie theatres. Most people though with 29.2% have a pretty undifferentiated opinion towards a possible future of the 3D technology and state that they either do not know or do not care about it at all.

3D - will become new trend soon	8,5%
3D - will become trend in couple of years	21,2%
3D - will remain huge in the theaters only	24,2%
3D -will become out-dated by another technology	16,1%
Don't know / Don't care	29,2%

(N=236)

TABLE 5 - WHERE THE TARGET GROUP SEES THE FUTURE OF 3D

We will have a look if the perception towards 3D TV changes with the degree of observability and trialability the target group encountered during the last 12 months. Therefore a Spearman correlation test is conducted:

			Watched 3D OWN TV	Watched 3D ELSES 3D TV	Watched 3D MOVIE THEATER	Haven't watched 3D at all
Spearman-Rho	General Opinion towards 3D	**Correlation Coefficient**	**,198**[**]	**-,053**	**,119**	**-,146**[*]
		Sig. (2-tailed)	,002	,406	,062	,021
		N	248	248	248	248

TABLE 6 - SPEARMAN CORRELATION: GERNERAL OPINION TOWARDS 3D AND TRIALABILITY OF 3D TV

Interesting to see is that even though there is a light and significant correlation between those people who have watched 3D on their own 3D TV and their general opinion towards the technology obviously – this statement is not valid for those who have watched 3D at someone else's TV, e.g. friends or co-workers. In fact there even seems to be a negative correlation between those two variables but the significance of 40% also shows that we cannot assume that there is any correlation – neither positive nor negative – at all. Regarding those who have watched 3D in the movie theaters there is a slightly positive correlation. In contrast – there is a negative correlation between the general opinion towards 3D and those people who have not seen 3D at all within the past 12 months. We can therefore assume that the trialability of 3D increases the general opinion towards 3D TV at least at some point.

RESEARCH QUESTION 4 – HOW EDUCATED IS THE TARGET GROUP ABOUT 3DTV?

The question of how educated the target group is refers solely on those people who do not have an own 3D TV, making out 245 respondents or 95% of the sample size.

In general the target group is mixed about their familiarity with the concept of 3D TV. 35.5% of them state to be either relatively or very familiar with the concept of 3D TV while 39.1% are relatively or very unfamiliar with it.

Familiarity with 3D TV

Very unfamiliar	Relatively unfamiliar	Heard of	Relatively familiar	Very familiar
42	54	62	51	36
17,1%	22,0%	25,3%	20,8%	14,7%

TABLE 7 - TARGET'S GROUP FAMILIARITY WITH 3D TV

Almost 50% of the respondents think that a complete 3D TV set costs between $1,000 and $2,000, which actually reflects a reasonable price for a set. 10.2% think that a price above $3,000 would be reasonable for a 3D TV while 18.6% think that they could buy a 3D TV for less than $1,000 (see table 23).

Very mixed are the responses also when the target group is asked about their familiarity with the fact that they can watch 2D content on a 3D TV. 28% have never heard of that while 28.4% are very familiar with that concept (see table 24 and graphic 13).

27.7% of the target group state that they have not watched any 3D content within the last 12 months, while 61.4% have seen at least one 3D movie in the movie theaters and 9.7% indicate they have been able to watch 3D TV at someone else's TV. The 6.8% that state they have seen 3D content somewhere else name especially retail store (such as BestBuy) that displays 3D content (see table 25).

According to the Spearman correlation test, as seen in the following graphic, there is a light positive correlation between the opinion towards 3D TV of the target group and their familiarity with this technology.

			General Opinion towards 3D	Familiarity with 3D TV
Spearman-Rho	General Opinion towards 3D	Spearman correlation coefficient	1,000	,103
		Sig. (2-taied)	.	,106
		N	248	248
	Familiarity with 3D TV	Spearman correlation coefficient	,103	1,000
		Sig. (2-tailed)	,106	.
		N	248	258

TABLE 8 - SPEARSON CORRELATION: GENERAL OPINION TOWARDS 3D AND FAMILIARITY WITH 3D TV

Interesting is also to examine whether the general opinion towards 3D TV has anything to do with different factors of education of the technology. Therefore a Spearman correlation test is carried out:

			General Opinion towards 3D	Awareness of 2D content on 3D TV
Spearman-Rho	General Opinion towards 3D	Spearman Correlation Coefficient	1,000	,218**
		Sig. (2-tailed)	.	,001
		N	248	248
	Awareness of 2D content on 3D TV	Spearman Correlation Coefficient	,218**	1,000
		Sig. (2-tailed)	,001	.
		N	248	248

**. The correlation is significant at level 0.01 (2-tailed).

TABLE 9 – SPEARMAN CORRELATION: GENERAL OPNINION TOWARDS 3D AND AWARENESS TO WATCH 2D CONTENT ON A 3D TV

As seen on this table there is a significant correlation between these two variables. The more aware the target group is of the fact that 3D display not only show 3D content but that they are also able to watch 2D shows on it, the more positive is their general opinion towards 3D TV.

RESEARCH QUESTION 5 – WHAT ARE THE OBSTACLES TO ADAPT TO 3D TV?

There is almost a 50:50 ratio of the target group when they are asked whether or not they consider the price for a 3D TV set as appropriate. However this price they are talking about is the price they personally think a 3D TV costs.

236 people answered the question what they see as the biggest weakness of 3D TV. A high majority of 43.2% stated the need to wear 3D glasses to watch 3D content, followed by 22% that do not see any added value to the 2D TV experience (see table 26).

		Should your next TV be a 3D TV?
<6months	%	3,7%
within the last year	%	25,9%
within the last two years	%	29,6%
>2 years	%	33,3%
Don't remember	%	7,4%

TABLE 10 – CROSSTAB: PURCHASE OF LAST TV AND DESIRE TO PURCHASE A 3D TV AS NEXT TV

Significant is that only 3.7% of the respondents who bought a TV within the last 6months are interested in a 3D TV as their next TV. The percentage increases the longer ago the purchase was. 1/3 of the respondents whose last purchase had been more than two years ago are interested in buying a 3D TV.

It was aimed to determine which factors would possibly increase the likeliness of the target group to buy a 3D TV in order to figure out whether those factors can be seen as obstacles. 63.1% of the respondents state that no need to wear 3D glasses would probably or definitely positively influence their likeliness to purchase a 3D TV. 65.2% would like a decrease of price and 55.1% would like more available 3D content.

Change opinion when no need to wear 3D glasses					
	Definitely not	*Probably not*	*Unsure*	*Probably yes*	*Definitely*
	29	20	37	68	81
	12,3%	8,5%	15,7%	28,8%	34,3%
Change opinion if prices decreased					
	Definitely not	*Probably not*	*Unsure*	*Probably yes*	*Definitely*
	23	19	37	65	89
	9,7%	8,1%	15,7%	27,5%	37,7%
Change opinion if there was more content available					
	Definitely not	*Probably not*	*Unsure*	*Probably yes*	*Definitely*
	31	24	47	66	64
	13,1%	10,2%	19,9%	28,0%	27,1%

TABLE 11 - OPINION-CHANGING FACTORS

ANALYSIS

After interpreting the target group research, the research questions now will be analyzed in order to answer the main question of the target group research.

ANALYSIS OF THE RESEARCH QUESTIONS

HOW ARE THE INNOVATORS OF THE 3D TV TECHNOLOGY CHARACTERIZED?

This question is important in order to figure out how the innovators of 3D TV are defined and with those the people with the highest likeliness to adapt to a new technology such as 3D TV.
In short, the definition is as followed: The innovators of 3D TV are male, childless, between 26 and 41 years, highly educated, work in the field of technology, engineering or computing and belong to the group of high-income earners.
3% of the conducted target group is considered to be an innovator of 3D TV.
Marketing activities for 3D TV should adapted to fit this profile as this group has not yet been tapped to its full potential and in order to increase the adoption rate it is recommended to focus on this group first.

The innovators enjoy watching 3D content such as movies and sports. Due to the fact that they are all males, it is not surprising, that 0% is interested in watching e.g. reality shows or series in 3D as those usually aim for a female target group.
In that regard, 3D content producers should focus to fulfill their interest concerning those genres, meaning that the production of 3D movies and the broadcasting of sport events in 3D should have priority.

As the group of innovators belongs to a high-income class, the price of a 3D TV does not play an important role. Even though half of the respondents named the technology to be inappropriately priced, it obviously did not hinder them from purchasing a 3D TV.
In accordance with Djolov's definition of the price skimming strategy, the prices of 3D therefore do not necessarily need to be decreased immediately as 3D TV has not yet reached out to the whole high-income segment.

WHAT IS THE TARGET GROUP'S TV VIEWING BEHAVIOR AND HOW AFFILIATED ARE THEY WITH THE TECHNOLOGY IN THE TV MARKET?

The majority of the target group possesses a TV – 90%. The majority of those has an HDTV and 25% are internet-connectable. The average person out of the sample watches less than 2h of TV every day and then it is mostly movies, documentaries or the news.

Around 22% of the target group purchased a new TV within the past two years. The Spearman correlation test showed that there is in fact a negative correlation between this variable and the target group's willingness to purchase a new TV within the next two years. That means that those that just recently bought a new TV are relatively unlikely to purchase a new TV soon. This is reflected in the fact that more than 65% of the respondents indicate that they will probably or definitely not buy a new TV within the next two years. Also the majority in fact states that they do not see a reason to buy a new TV as they are satisfied with the one they already have.

For most people a lack in interest in technology does not play a significant role when it comes down to their buying behavior. Only 18% state that they are not interested in new technology in the TV market. Actually, 40% would buy an HDTV as their next TV, 31% even want their new TV to be internet-connectable and 10% fancy a 3D TV. Though this number does not necessarily reflect a high interest in 3D, it still shows that the target group indeed is interested in the technology that is available and those 10% might make out the early adopters of 3D TV.

Most people bought their TV more than two years ago but around one fifth bought it within the last 12 months. The Pearson correlation showed that there is negative correlation between the time of the last TV purchase and the willingness of the target group to buy a new TV within the next two years. That shows, that indeed the introduction of HDTVs and the broad adoption if it may act as an obstacle for the 3D TVs. As most people adapted to HDTVs and therefore bought a new TV not that long ago, they do not see a reason right now to purchase a new TV soon. That is also reflected in the reasons they mention. A vast majority of 60% is satisfied with their TV and does not see any reason to buy another one anytime soon.

However - contradictory to the target group's interest in new technology, their willingness to spend money on it is comparatively low. Half of them want to spend a maximum of $500 for a new TV and less than 10% would pay more than $1,000. The more money they are willing to invest has a slight correlation with the probability to buy a new TV within the next two year. Therefore we can conclude that financial issues of the target group at this moment might be a reason for not buying a new TV and that might become an important factor for the adoption of 3D.

10% of the target group say that they want their next TV to be a 3D TV and more than half of the respondents value the increased engagement into the action by watching 3D content as the biggest advantage of this technology.
The opinion of the target group towards 3D TV is generally undifferentiated but with a larger part tending to have a rather negative perception. But despite that, almost 30% believe that 3D will become a new trend within a couple of years.

It was examined how the target group's perception changes with their increased level of trialability/observability. As there is a positive correlation between the perceptions of those who have watched 3D on their own TV towards the technology, we can assume that the innovators of 3D TV are satisfied with their purchase.
On the contrary, people who have watched 3D TV on someone else's 3D TV set, tend to be more negative towards it even though the data shows that there is no relevant significance between those two variables.
People however that have watched 3D in the movie theatres are more likely to think positive about 3D TV, whereas those who have not watched any 3D content at all within the past 12 months, are more negative about it.
Though the gathered data do not show a high correlation between the different variables, in general we can conclude that the perception of 3D improves with the degree of trialability and observability.

HOW EDUCATED IS THE TARGET GROUP ABOUT 3D TV?

A main obstacle that has to be overcome in order to make 3D TV successful is the education of target group in regards to the 3D technology. Only if they understand the developments that this technology goes through there is a chance that they will adapt to it.
In general, the target group is kind of familiar with the 3D TV technology as 35% state to be either relatively or very familiar with it. 17% however indicate to be very unfamiliar with it.
The majority of the target group does know approximately how much a 3D TV set cost, so think more than 50% that it is between $1,000 and $2,000. That shows that they do actually know very well how much a 3D TV set costs.

Even though the target group's knowledge about the fact that they can watch 2D content on a 3D display is very ambivalent, the Spearman correlation test shows that the higher this awareness, the more positive the perception of the target group is towards 3D.
Another Spearman correlation test shows that there is some degree of correlation between the question of how familiar the target group is with 3D and the opinion they have about it.

This shows that a consumer who is well-informed about the technology will probably have a better perception of the technology.

WHAT ARE THE OBSTACLES TO ADAPT TO 3D TV?

As seen in the previous question, a majority of the target group is well educated about the current prices of 3D TV sets, but if it comes to prices, we see an obstacle for the consumer – almost 50% think that this price is not appropriate for a 3D TV.
When the target group was asked whether or not decreased prices would change their opinion about 3D TV, 65% state that it would definitely or probably do so. We see in here that the prices indeed are an important factor for the adoption of 3D TV.
However, the price was not the most mentioned weakness of 3D TV, in fact it were the needed glasses with more than 43%, 22% state that they do not see the added value of 3D TV compared to the traditional 2D experience.

Also as mentioned earlier, the launch-date of the technology had probably been unfavorable. We've seen that there is a negative correlation between the purchase of the last TV and the probability of buying a new TV within the next two years. Additionally we see that among those who bought TV within the past year, about 30% are interested in purchasing a 3D TV, while this percentage increases the longer ago their last purchase had been.

As 3D glasses had been named the number one weakness of 3D technology, the target group was asked whether their perception would change if no glasses needed to be involved in order to watch 3D TV and indeed 63% would probably or definitely change their opinion in that case.
In the case of available content, for 55% more content would positively influence their perception of 3D TV.

What we can conclude from that is that the launch date of 3D TV indeed has been a huge obstacle for the technology and even though prices might not play a big role for the innovators of 3D TV, they do for the general target group. But what irritates the consumer the most is still the need to wear glasses in order to watch 3D content.

HOW DOES THE TARGET GROUP'S PERCEPTION TOWARDS 3D TV INFLUENCE THE ADOPTION RATE OF 3D TV?

According to E. Rogers (2003), the adoption rate is influenced by different characteristics that have already been analyzed in the light of the market research. The target group research gives an indication into how the target group's perception influences the adoption of 3D TV.

RELATIVE ADVANTAGE

The extra value that the added experience domain of 3D creates is an increased feeling of engagement into the action of the 3D content. This is the unique selling point - and indeed the target group sees that point as the major advantage of the 3D technology. However a large percentage also does not see any added value of 3D compared to 2D.

Even though price is not an important factor for innovators of 3D TV, it does play a significant role for the target group in general. The study shows that a decreased price of the technology would lead to an increased perception of it. With the majority of the target group willing to pay only a maximum of $500 makes the probability of them to purchase a 3D TV that costs at least twice that much very low. The financial situation of the target group therefore negatively affects the adoption rate of 3D TV. However, as it is still a new technology on the market, prices are likely to drop even further and with that reaching out to the 50% of the target group that is not willing to pay that much for a 3D TV.

COMPATIBILITY

The target group shows that 3D TV indeed had an unfavorable launch date. The longer ago the last purchase of their TV was the higher their interest in buying a 3D TV and also the higher the probability of buying a TV within the next two years. As 44% of the target group already purchased a TV within the past two years the possibility of those 44% to purchase a 3D TV anytime soon is very low. The launching date is therefore an important factor in the adoption of 3D TV that probably leads to a delayed adoption process for a major part of the target group.

Furthermore is the need to wear glasses seen as the biggest disadvantage of 3D TV, incompatible with the values of the target group. The perception of 3D TV would drastically increase if there was no need to wear glasses for 3D TV.

Most of the 3D content that is released are 3D movies, also a lot of sports event are broadcasting in 3D - such as the 2010 World Cup. This fact has a high compatibility with the target group's interest in 3D content, as they want to see especially movies, documentaries and sports events.

The majority of the target group possesses a TV – 90%. This actually reflects the percentage of the whole population. However, nowadays you would probably expect this number to be higher. This might be explained by the digital revolution that changed the role of the TV in general. Due to broadband internet and online video-on-demand services, a TV set is not the only medium to watch TV anymore. As many respondents of the target group mentioned, they use their computers to stream their favorite shows or movies. As we are talking about a young target group with a high percentage of students, this might explain the reason for the fact that "only" 90% of them actually have a TV.

COMPLEXITY

Though 3D is and will stay a rather complex technology as long as there is no standardized technology, the target group seems to be well-educated about the technology and their functions, so that the complex technology does not play a significant role in the adoption process of 3D TV.

TRIALABILITY/OBSERVABILITY

The level of trialability and observability is so far low among the target group, if it is restricted to watch 3D TV, as only a small percentage has access to watch 3D TV if it is not in some retail store. But the level of trialability/observability remains high when it comes to movie theatres. 60% of the target group have seen some 3D movies within the past 12 months. The results show that people who watched 3D in the theaters have a better perception of the technology than the ones who did not. As more and more 3D movies are launched, the perception of 3D will increase among the target group. As there is a positive correlation between the perception and the interest in purchasing a 3D TV, we can assume that this will lead to a higher adoption rate of 3D TVs.

PART 3 - CONCLUSION & DISCUSSION

The main aim of this research is to determine whether or not 3D TV will be able to increase its adoption and become successful within the next three to five years.

The market research in part one showed how several characteristics influence the adoption and how those can be used in order to improve the adoption. Part 2, the target group research, was testing the probability of those assumptions under the light of the target group's perception towards both TV in general and 3D TV specifically. After analyzing the two research parts we can now come up with a conclusion in order to answer the main question of the research.

First of all the relative advantage: Obviously the immersion of the consumer while watching 3D content is the unique selling point of 3D TV leading to an increased engagement into the action. Research showed that even though the consumer is aware of this fact, this UPS fails to create a new value for the consumer. The added experience of 3D TV in comparison to 2D is not yet valued enough by the target group in order to convince them of this new technology.

Despite the experience factor though, the adoption could be increased by a decrease in price. The 3D TV technology is still very innovative and new, that means that the prices are likely to decrease even more within the next couple of months. In that case, 3D TV will be able to reach out to the next segment of the consumer and increase its adoption.

Glasses so far have been the biggest obstacle of the consumer to adapt to 3D TV because they are expensive, uncomfortable and not to use with other brands. The change to universal glasses and/or passive glasses however is the first step to overcome this obstacle. At some point, with the introduction of auto-stereoscopic 3D displays worldwide, 3D glasses will become unnecessary and this will definitely boost the 3D market if the price is right for this technology.

The launching date of 3D had been unfavorable, which was proven on several occasions. This fact in addition to the consumer's wait-and-see approach and the delay of gratification negatively influences the adoption of 3D.

Negative influence also results from the digital revolution that changed the media consumption of the consumer from TV to computers with the use of the internet.

The development on the 3D TV market – new movies in 3D, sports events broadcasted in 3D and broadcasting channels launching their 3D channels – supplements the consumer's interest in watching specific content in 3D and therefore increases the 3D adoption.

The level of trialability and observability is so far low among the target group, if it is restricted to watch 3D TV, as only a small percentage has access to watch 3D TV if it is not in some retail store. But the level of trialability/observability remains high when it comes to movie theatres. 60% of the target group has seen some 3D movies within the past 12 months

Another very important aspect that influences the adoption rate in almost every aspect is the degree of education of the target group about the 3D TV technology. The target group needs to know about the technology on the market in order to build their own opinion about it. The target group research showed that the consumer indeed is educated about the different aspects of 3D TVs and showed a positive correlation between the degree of education and the perception towards 3D TV. As another test showed that there is also a positive correlation between perception and willingness to purchase a 3D TV we can conclude that education is the key point in making 3D successful.

According to the market research together with the target group research, the future of 3D seems to be positive. Even though it came at a time in which most people do not see the need for a new TV in general, but in the course of the years this will change and people will buy a new TV. At this time due to the high competition in the 3D market, the available 3D TVs will be highly diverse in order to fulfill different needs and expectations. The prices will probably drop even further, reaching out to other segments of the population and making it easier for the broad mass to purchase a 3D TV.

3D will probably have its breakthrough as soon as auto-stereoscopic 3D will be available to an affordable price. Unfortunately we do not know when this will be the case. All the signs suggest that this will probably not happen within the next 5 years as this technology is too new and too expensive at the moment. So the people that can really not endure the thought of wearing glasses in order to watch TV will have to wait for some more time.

But in order to make 3D TV successful among the target group an important aspect is education about the technology. Throughout the research it became clear that to educate the target group about the 3D technology is the key factor to success. The target group research showed that so far the degree of education positively influences the success of 3D TV. Therefore a major task for 3D TV manufacturers should be to focus their marketing activities into educating the target group. But education is also important for the 3D content producers. They need to bear in mind that 3D is a gimmick to the TV experience and not a whole new experience. The focus needs to be on producing good content in order to make a movie or a show successful and not on technology.

Nevertheless it has to be taken into account that the conducted target group research is based on a non-representative sample of the population and the indicated results might therefore be biased. In order to get a valid result, it is recommended to repeat the target group research, using a representative sample in order to prove the results of this research right or wrong.

Active 3D - Two different pictures are shown (one for each eye), a transmitter synchronizes the 3D display with the active shutter glasses in which the shutters close and open again very fast, so that each eye only sees the picture that it is supposed to see. The glasses have a very high refresh rate, but flickering can occur, causing headaches or nausea. Requires bulky and expensive glasses and an additional transmitter for the complete 3D experience.

Anaglyph images - 3D effect created by using color filters (usually red & cyan). By wearing corresponding glasses the two images are separated for the eyes creating a 3D effect.

Auto stereoscopy - The method of creating a 3D effect without the need of special glasses

Delay of Gratification - The ability of an individual to waive an immediate reward or pleasure for a more essential reward or pleasure in the future.

Passive 3D - 3D technology that used polarized glasses that are cheap and comfortable. Instead of the glasses separating actively the pictures for each eye, a thin polarized layer on the passive 3D display does that by splitting the images according to the polarization of the glasses. This results in a brighter image but also cuts the resolution in half compared to active displays.

PESTEL Analysis - A framework to analyze political, economic, social, technological, environmental and legal factors. It is a framework to determine external factors that have to be taken into consideration.

Stereoscopy - Umbrella term for any technique to create three-dimensional content by presenting two slightly different pictures separately to the eyes of the viewer (e.g. active 3D, passive 3D, anaglyph 3D)

Streaming - Transferring data (such as music or video) whereas the content can be watched/listened to while the data is transmitted to the user. There is no need to download the content to the computer and wait until the download is finished before the user can access the file. Widely used for live-broadcasting via the internet (internet radio, internet TV) or Video on Demand (VoD) services.

SOURCES

BOOKS

DJOLOV, G. (2006). *The Economics of Competition. The Race to Monopoly.*
London: The Haworth Press

HEERINK, M. (2006). *Praktische Schrijfgids*
Amsterdam: Pearson Education

JOHNSON, G., SCHOLES, K. & WHITTINGTON, R. (2008). *Exploring Corporate Strategy*, 8th edition. Harlow: Pearson Prentice Hall

MENDIBURU, B. (2009). *3D Movie Making - Stereoscopic Digital Cinema from Script to Screen.* Burlington: Focal Press.

NIJS, D. & PETERS, F. (2006). *Imagineering. Het creëren van belevingswerelden.*
Amsterdam: Uitgeverij Boom.

OOSTERBAAN, W. (1995). *Het schrijven van een leesbare scriptie*
Rotterdam: NRC Handelsblad

PINE J. & GILMORE, J. (1999). *The experience economy: work is theatre & every business a stage.*
Boston: Harvard Business School Press.

ROGERS, E. (2003). *Diffusion of Innovations*, 5th edition.
New York: The Free Press.

SAUNDERS, M., LEWIS, P. & THORNHILL, A. (2004) *Methoden en technieken van onderzoek*, 3rd ed.
Amsterdam: Pearson Prentice Hall.

ZONE, R. (2007). *Stereoscopic Cinema and the origins of 3-D film, 1838 - 1952.*
Kentucky: The University Press of Kentucky

EBOOKS

EARL, J. (2010). *3D-TV – Is It For You?* [Kindle DX Version]
retrieved from Amazon.com

REPORTS

Central Intelligence Agency. The *World Factbook – United States*
Last modified on May 17, 2011, retrieved May 19, 2011 via
https://www.cia.gov/library/publications/the-world-factbook/geos/us.html
market

Display Search – NPD Group Company. *Quarterly TV Design and Features Report.* 2011
http://www.displaysearch.com/cps/rde/xchg/displaysearch/hs.xsl/quarterly_tv_desig n_features_report.asp

Display Search. *3D TV Forecast to Reach 3.2 Million Global Shipments in 2010 and 91 Million in 2014.* January 4, 2011
http://www.displaysearch.com/cps/rde/xchg/displaysearch/hs.xsl/110104_3d_tv_fore cast_to_reach_3_2_million_global_shipments_in_2010_and_91_million_in_2014.asp

EVANS, S. for Harris Interactive. *Harris Buzz Report. Report #2.* October 2010
http://www.harrisinteractive.com/vault/HI_UK_TMT_REPORT_Buzz-Report2-2010-10.pdf

Renub Research. *3D TV Market and Future Forecast Worldwide (2010 - 2014)*; January 19, 2011 retrieved via
http://www.marketresearch.com/product/display.asp?productid=6066446, Publication ID RNBR6066446

The Nielsen Company. *State of the Media 2010. U.S. Audiences and Devices.* January 5, 2011
http://blog.nielsen.com/nielsenwire/wp-content/uploads/2011/01/nielsen-media-fact-sheet-jan-11.pdf

The Nielsen Company. *Purchase Intent for 3DTV Varies Around the Globe.* December 20, 2010
http://blog.nielsen.com/nielsenwire/consumer/purchase-intent-for-3dtv-varies-around-the-globe/

US CENSUS BUREAU

HUMES, K., JONES, N., RAMIREZ, R.: *Overview of Race and Hispanic Origin: 2010 - 2010 Census Briefs* (March 2011)
http://www.census.gov/prod/cen2010/briefs/c2010br-02.pdf, retrieved May 19, 2011

MACKUN, P., WILSON, S.: *Population Distribution and Change: 2000 to 2010 – 2010 Census Briefs* (March 2011)
http://www.census.gov/prod/cen2010/briefs/c2010br-01.pdf, retrieved May 19, 2011

U.S. Census Bureau. *State & County QuickFacts – USA.* Last modified on November 4, 2010
http://quickfacts.census.gov/qfd/states/00000.html, retrieved March 14, 2011

ARTICLES

TV marketers face a tougher time than their theatrical peers selling consumers on 3D. (January 1, 2011) in: Entertainment Marketing Letter, Volume 24, page 1. ISSN: 1048-5112, retrieved via www.nexis.com on February 28, 2011

Universiteit van Tilburg. *Bronvermelding volgens de richtlijnen van de APA.* (December 2010)
Tilburg: Library and IT Services.
retrieved via
http://drcwww.uvt.nl/its/voorlichting/handleidingen/bibliotheek/apa.pdf on June 4, 2011

ONLINE ARTICLES

www.articlesbase.com: n.a.: *An Introduction To 3D Television* (April 8, 2010)
http://www.articlesbase.com/cable-and-satellite-tv-articles/an-introduction-to-3d-television-2118793.html, retrieved April 29, 2011

www.boxofficemojo.com: n.a.: *All Time Box Office – Worldwide Grosses* (n.d.)
http://boxofficemojo.com/alltime/world, retrieved March 18, 2011

www.business-sites.philips.com: n.a.: *What is 3D?* (n.d.)
http://www.business-sites.philips.com/sites/philipsbs/3dsolutions/3dcontentinterfaceformats/whatis3d/index.page, retrieved March 7, 2011

www.cablefax.com: ROBERTS, S.: *All I want for Christmas?: 3DTV Adoption Has Lots of Room to Run.* (December 16, 2010)
www.cablefax.com/cfp/xfax/program/44441.html, retrieved May 4, 2011

ezinearticles.com: OSHANNESSY, M: *3D TV - Has the Bubble Burst or Has It Just Gone Momentarily Pear Shaped?* (November 16, 2010)
http://ezinearticles.com/?3D-TV---Has-the-Bubble-Burst-or-Has-It-Just-Gone-Momentarily-Pear-Shaped?&id=5387957, retrieved March 7, 2011

www.homemediamagazine.com: TRIBBEY, C: *3D Summit: Consumers Not Willing To Pay Much More For 3D At Home* (September 17, 2009) http://www.homemediamagazine.com/3-d/3d-summit-consumers-not-willing-to-pay-much-more-for-3d-at-home-17088, retrieved March 7, 2011

www.hothardware.com: LILLY, P: Toshiba *Reportedly on Pace to Launch First Glasses-Free 3D TV* (August 24, 2010) http://hothardware.com/News/Toshiba-Reportedly-on-Pace-to-Launch-First-GlassesFree-3D-TV, retrieved May 4, 2011

www.informationweek.com: SHEIN, E.: *3D TVs Fail to Draw Holiday Shoppers.* (December 15, 2010) http://www.informationweek.com/news/global-cio/interviews/228800642, retrieved May 4, 2011

mashable.com: SNIDERMAN, Z.: *How Does 3D Technology Work?* (February 7, 2011) http://mashable.com/2011/02/07/how-does-3d-work/ , retrieved March 7, 2011

www.mediacollege.com: n.a.: *What is 3D?* (n.d.) www.mediacollege.com/3d/intro.html, retrieved March 7, 2011

www.novagazette.com: n.a.: *Latest 3DTV Viewing Research Finds Consumer Interest High, Yet Tempered with Concerns about 3D Glasses and Inability to Multitask* (November 19, 2010) http://novagazette.com/latest-3dtv-viewing-research-finds-consumer-interest-high-yet-tempered-with-concerns-about-3d-glasses-and-inability-to-multitask, retrieved May 4, 2011

www.pcmag.com: GREENWALD, W.: *RealD Announces Universal 3D Glasses Technology.* (January 6, 2011) http://www.pcmag.com/article2/0,2817,2375295,00.asp, retrieved March 21, 2011

www.stern.de: SANDER, R.: *"Avatar" - das Comeback der 3D-Technik. Hollywood will nicht mehr flach sein* (December 16, 2009) http://www.stern.de/digital/homeentertainment/2-avatar-das-comeback-der-3d-technik-hollywood-will-nicht-mehr-flach-sein-1529910.html, retrieved March 7, 2011

weblogs.dailypress.com: WERNER, L.: *Passive 3D TV: Consumer Reports weighs in on the latest.* (February 7, 2011) http://weblogs.dailypress.com/features/shoppingblog/2011/02/3d_tv_consumer_reports_weighs.html, retrieved March 21, 2011

PRESENTATIONS

GAGNON, P. *3D TV Forecast Outlook.* (Presentation hold at the 2009 3D Entertainment Summit in Los Angeles, California) http://www.3d-summit.com/Upload/Content/Documents/Paul%20Gagnon.pdf

APPENDIX

APPENDIX 1 - GRAPHICS

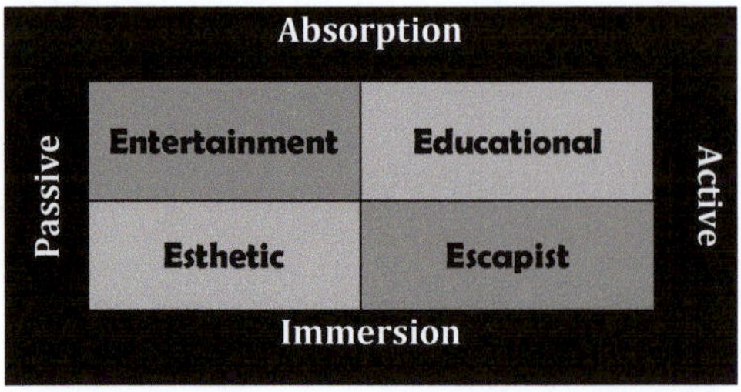

GRAPHIC 5- THE FOUR EXPERIENCE DOMAINS ACCORDING TO PINE & GILMORE

Graphic adapted from PINE J. & GILMORE, J. (1999). *The experience economy: work is theatre & every business a stage.* Boston: Harvard Business School Press.

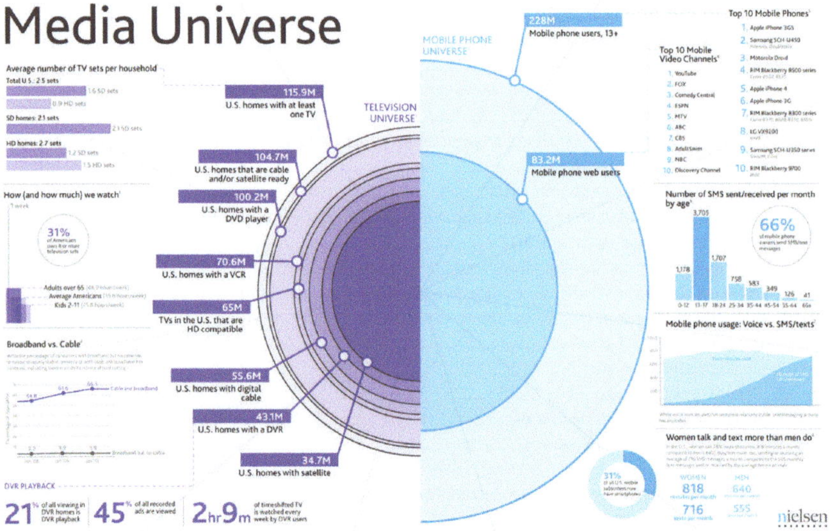

GRAPHIC 6 - NIELSEN NATIONAL PEOPLE METER

Graphic taken from The Nielsen Company. *State of the Media 2010. U.S. Audiences and Devices.* January 5, 2011

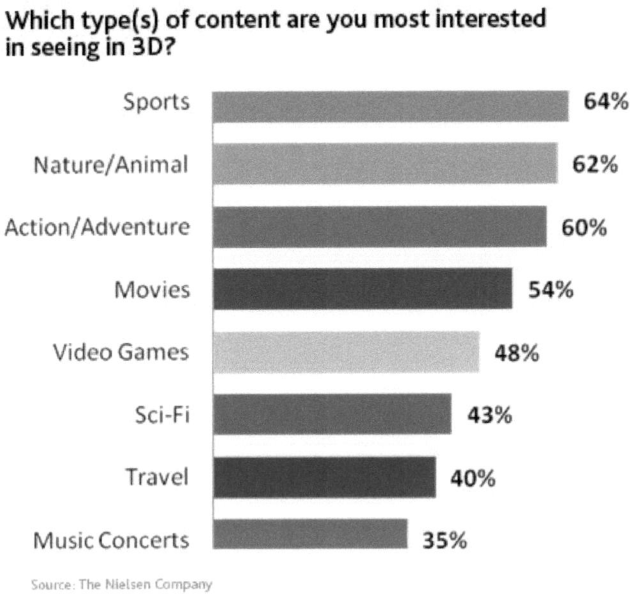

GRAPHIC 7 - MOST FAVORITE TYPE OF CONTENT

Graphic by The Nielsen Company, 2010

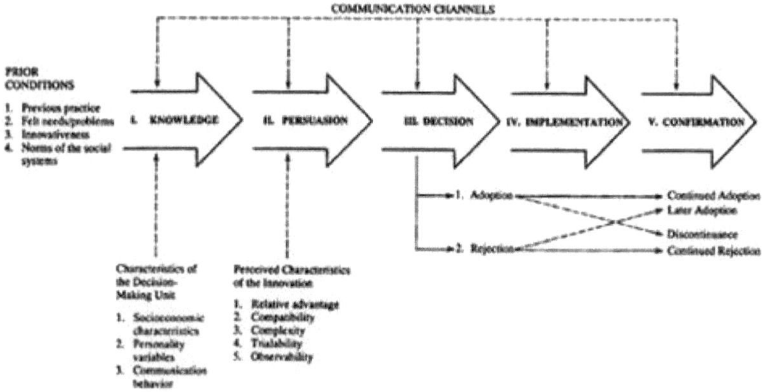

GRAPHIC 8 - ADOPTION PROCESS ACCORDING TO E. ROGERS

Graphic used from ROGERS, E. (2003). *Diffusion of Innovations*, 5th edition. New York: The Free Press.

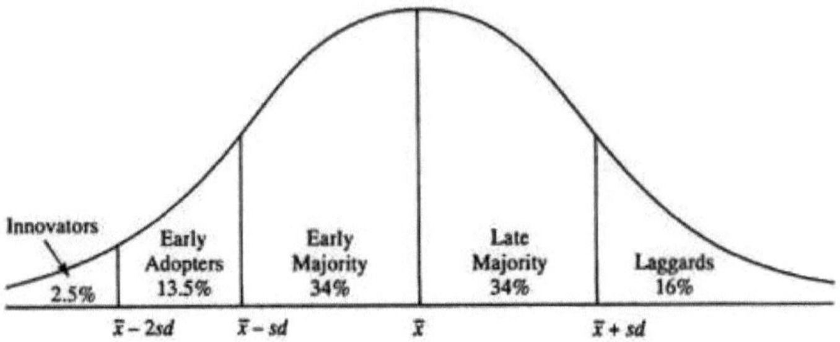

GRAPHIC 9 - ADOPTER CATEGORIZATION ACCORDING TO E. ROGERS

Graphic used from ROGERS, E. (2003). *Diffusion of Innovations,* 5th edition. New York: The Free Press.

Age	%
0	,4
<18	,7
18-25	35,0
26-33	35,0
34-41	12,8
42-50	6,6
51-58	4,0
58-65	4,7
>65	,7
Total (N=274)	100,0

TABLE 12 - AGE DISTRIBUTION OF SAMPLE

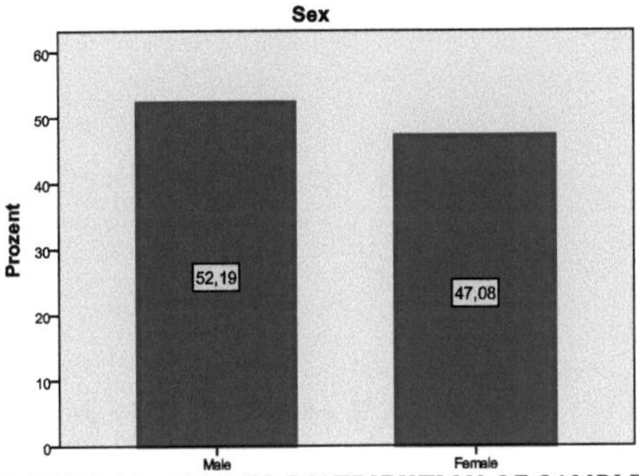

GRAPHIC 10 - GENDER DISTRIBUTION OF SAMPLE

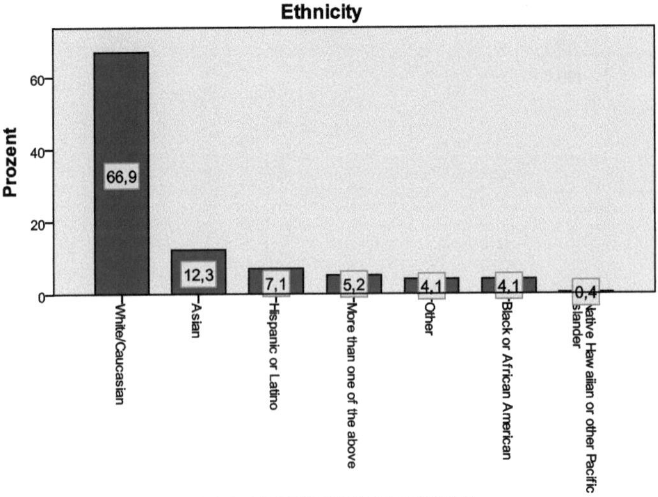

GRAPHIC 11 - ETHNIC DISTRIBUTION OF SAMPLE

Occupation	%
Administrative/Secretarial	3,3
Artist/Creative/Performance	6,6
Executive/Management	6,6
Financial Service	4,0
Homemaker	1,1
Labor/Construction	,4
Legal	1,8
Medical/Dental/Veterinary	2,6
Retail/Food Service	3,3
Sales/Marketing	5,9
Student	19,9
Teacher/Professor	8,5
Technical/Computers/Engineering	15,4
Travel/Hospitality/Transportation	1,5
Other	19,1
Total (N=272)	**100,0**

TABLE 13 - OCCUPATIONAL BACKGROUND OF SAMPLE

Age	%
18-25	1 12,5%
26-33	3 37,5%
34-41	2 25,0%
51-58	1 12,5%
58-65	1 12,5%

TABLE 14 - AGE DISTRIBUTION OF 3D INNOVATORS

Annual Income	%
<$25,000	12,5%
$35,001 - $50,000	25,0%
$50,001 - $75,000	25,0%
$150,000+	37,5%

TABLE 15 - ANNUAL INCOME OF 3D INNOVATORS

Occupation	%
Artist/Creative/Performance	12,5%
Legal	25,0%
Sales/Marketing	12,5%
Student	12,5%
Technical/Computers/Engineering	37,5%

TABLE 16 - OCCUPATIONAL BACKGROUND OF 3D INNOVATORS

Amount of TVs	%
0	10,3
1	41,6
2	25,1
3	11,5
4	7,4
4+	4,1
Total (N=243)	

TABLE 17 - AMOUNT OF TVS PER HOUSEHOLD OF THE TARGET GROUP

HD %	Plasma %	LCD %	Internet %	3D %
52,3	17,1	31,8	24,8	3,5

TABLE 18 - AVAILABLE TV TECHNOLOGY IN TARGET GROUP'S HOUSEHOLDS

	%
Definitely not	34,9
Probably not	31,0
Undecided	14,7
Somewhat likely	12,4
Definitely	6,6
Total (N=258)	100,0

TABLE 19 - TARGET GROUP'S PROBABILITY TO PURCHASE A NEW TV WITHIN THE NEXT 2 YEARS

No Need %	Financial %	No interest in technology %	Other %
59,7	22,9	18,2	10,1

TABLE 20 - TARGET GROUP'S REASON TO NOT PURCHASE A NEW TV WITHIN THE NEXT 2 YEARS

HD %	Internet %	3D %
40,7	31,4	10,4

TABLE 21 - TV TECHNOLOGY THE TARGET GROUP IS INTERESTED IN

	Frequency	Procent
<$250	63	24,9
$251 - $500	64	25,3
$501 - $1,000	81	32,0
$1,001 - $1,500	22	8,7
$1,501 - $2,000	16	6,3
$2,001 - $2,500	3	1,2
$2,501 - $3,000	3	1,2
$3,001 - $3,500	1	,4
(N=253)	253	100,0

TABLE 22 - POSSIBLE AMOUNT THE TARGET GROUP IS WILLING TO INVEST INTO A NEW TV

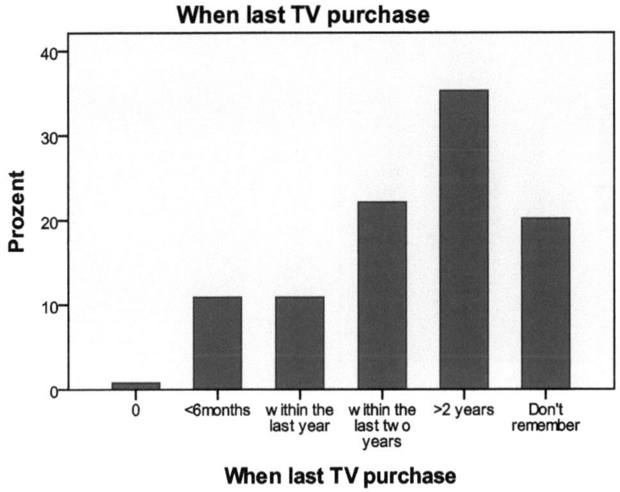

GRAPHIC 12 - LAST TV PURCHASE OF THE TARGET GROUP

How much do you think a 3D TV set costs?

<$250	$251 - $500	$501 - $1,000	$1,001 - $1,500	$1,501 - $2,000	$2,001 - $2,500	$2,501 - $3,000	$3,001 - $3,500	>$3,501
2	9	33	57	59	35	17	12	12
,8%	3,8%	14,0%	24,2%	25,0%	14,8%	7,2%	5,1%	5,1%

TABLE 23 - TARGET GROUP'S KNOWLEDGE ABOUT 3D TV SET PRICES

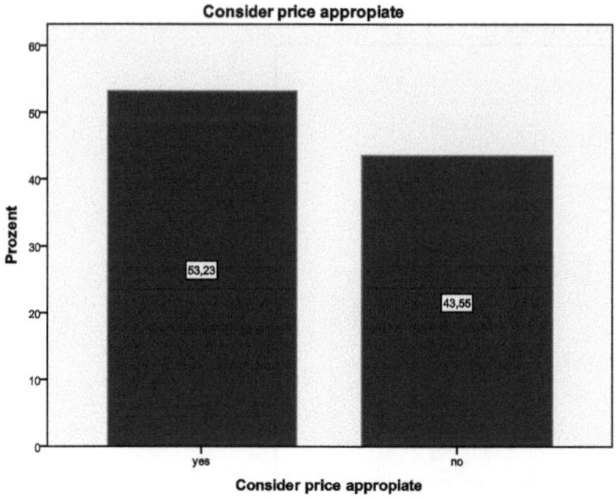

GRAPHIC 13 - OPINION OF TARGET GROUP ABOUT PRICE FOR 3D TV

Awareness of 2D content to be watched on a 3D TV

Never heard of	Relatively unfamiliar	Little bit familiar	Relatively familiar	Very familiar
66	30	34	39	67
28,0%	12,7%	14,4%	16,5%	28,4%

TABLE 24 - TARGET GROUP'S EDUCATION ABOUT THE FACT THAT 3D DISPLAYS ARE ALSO ABLE TO SHOW 2D COTENT

Someone elses' 3D TV	**Movie Theater**	**Somewhere else**	**Don't remember**	**Haven't watched 3D TV**
9,7	61,4	6,8	1,7	27,7

TABLE 25 - CHANNELS VIA WHICH THE TARGET GROUP WATCHED 3D WITHIN THE LAST 12 MONTHS

Greatest Weakness of 3D TV

Need to wear glasses	High costs	Lack of content	No added value to 2D experience	Other
102	38	19	52	25
43,2%	16,1%	8,1%	22,0%	10,6%

TABLE 26 - GREATEST WEAKNESS OF 3D TV ACCORDING TO THE TARGET GROUP

1. Age

- o <18
- o 18-25
- o 26-33
- o 34-41
- o 42-50
- o 51-58
- o 59-65
- o >65

2. Sex

- o Male
- o Female

3. State of Residence

____

4. Ethnicity

- o American Indian or Alaska Native
- o Asian
- o Black or African American
- o Hispanic or Latino
- o Native Hawaiian or other Pacific Islander
- o White/Caucasian
- o Other
- o More than one of the above

5. Highest Education Level

- o High School Graduate
- o Vocational/Technical School
- o Some college
- o Bachelor's Degree
- o Master's Degree
- o Doctorate/PhD
- o Other

6. Occupation

- Administrative/Secretarial
- Artist/Creative/Performance
- Executive/Management
- Financial Service
- Homemaker
- Labor/Construction
- Legal
- Medical/Dental/Veterinary
- Retail/Food Service
- Sales/Marketing
- Student
- Teacher/Professor
- Technical/Computers/Engineering
- Travel/Hospitality/Transportation
- Other

7. Household Size

- 1
- 2
- 3
- 4
- 5
- 5+

8. Annual Household Income

- Less than $25,000
- $25,001 to $35,000
- $35,001 to $50,000
- $50,001 to $75,000
- $75,000 to $100,000
- $100,001 to $150,000
- $150,001+
- Prefer not to answer

9. Number of children under 18 living in the same household

- 0
- 1
- 2
- 3
- 3+

10. How many TVs do you have in your household?

- 0
- 1
- 2
- 3
- 4
- 4+

11. How many hours per day do you spend watching TV approximately?

- <1h
- 1-2h
- 3-4h
- 5-6h
- 7-8h
- >8h

12. What type of content do you find usually watch? (multiple answers possible)

- Movies
- Documentaries (such as travel, nature or wild life documentaries)
- Music events/concerts
- Sports events
- Animation
- News
- Series
- Other, please specify: ___________

13. Which of the following characteristics does your TV have? (multiple answers possible)

- HD display
- Plasma display
- LCD display
- Internet connectivity
- 3D ability
- None of the above

14. When did you purchase your last TV?

- < 6 months
- Within the last year
- Within the last two years
- > than two years ago
- I don't remember

15. How much money are you willing to invest in your next TV?

- <$250
- $251 - $500
- $501 - $1000
- $1001 - $1500
- $1501 - $2000
- $2001 - $2500
- $2501 - $3000
- $3000-$3500
- >$3500

16. Are you likely to purchase a new TV within the next 24months?

definitely not	somewhat unlikely	undecided	somewhat likely	Definitely
❍	❍	❍	❍	❍

17. If you are unlikely to purchase a new TV within the next 24months, please state your reasons (multiple answers possible)

- Satisfied with current TV / no need to buy another one
- No financial resources
- No interest in new technology available on the market
- Other, please specify: __________

18. If you are likely to purchase a new TV within the next 24months, please state what characteristics it should have (multiple answers possible)

- o Undecided
- o HDTV
- o Internet-connectivity
- o 3D ability
- o Other, please specify: ____________

19. How familiar are you with the concept of 3D TV?

Never heard of	Relatively unfamiliar	Little bit familiar	Relatively familiar	Very familiar
○	○	○	○	○

20. Do you or a member of your household possess a 3D TV?

- o Yes, myself
- o Yes, another member of my household
- o No

21. Do you know anyone who has a 3D TV (e.g. family, friends, co-workers,...)?

- o Yes, friend(s) of mine
- o Yes, someone in my family
- o Yes, co-workers / other contacts
- o No
- o I don't know

22. How would you describe your general opinion towards 3D TV?

Very negative	negative	undifferentiated	positive	Very positive
○	○	○	○	○

23. How much do you think does the purchase of a complete 3D TV set cost? (including everything needed to watch 3D)

- o <$250
- o $251 - $500
- o $501 - $1000
- o $1001 - $1500
- o $1501 - $2000
- o $2001 - $2500
- o $2501 - $3000
- o $3000-$3500
- o >$3500

24. Do you consider this price as appropriate for the purchase of 3D TV?

- o yes
- o no

25. In your opinion, what do you think is the greatest advantage of 3D TV?

- o Picture quality
- o The cost-price ratio
- o It makes me feel more like being a part of the action
- o Other, please specify: ______________________________

26. What is according to your perception the greatest weakness of 3D TV?

- o The need to wear glasses
- o High costs
- o Lack of content
- o It doesn't add anything to the usual 2D TV experience
- o Other, please specify: _____________________

27. Are you aware of the fact that you can also watch regular 2D content 3D TV in HD quality?

Never heard of	Relatively unfamiliar	Little bit familiar	Relatively familiar	Very familiar
❍	❍	❍	❍	❍

28. Would the following scenarios positively influence your readiness to purchase a 3D TV?

	Definitely not	somewhat unlikely	undecided	somewhat likely	Definitely
No need to wear glasses	❍	❍	❍	❍	❍
Decreased prices	❍	❍	❍	❍	❍
More availale content	❍	❍	❍	❍	❍

29. Have you watched any 3D content within the past 12months? (multiple answers possible)

- o Yes, on my own 3D TV

- Yes, on someone else's 3D TV
- Yes, in the movie theatres
- No
- I don't remember
- Somewhere else (please specify): ____________

30. What type of content do you find the most interesting to watch in 3D? (multiple answers possible)

- 3D movies (e.g. Avatar, Tron,...)
- Documentaries (such as travel, nature or wild life documentaries)
- Music events/concerts
- Sports events
- Animation
- News
- Series
- Other, please specify: __________

31. Where do you personally see the 3D TVs in the future?

- 3D will become a new trend pretty soon
- 3D will eventually become pretty big in a couple of years
- 3D will remain big in the movie theatres only
- 3D will pretty soon become out-dated by another more advanced technology
- I don't know / I don't care

32. Additional comments/remarks about the topic:

____
____
____
____
____